"Our wishes are the true touchstones of our estate; such as we wish to be we are. Worldy hearts affect earthly things: spiritual, divine. We cannot better know what we are than by what we could be."
—Joseph Hall, English bishop

the wish list

by BARBARA ANN KIPFER

WORKMAN PUBLISHING

Library of Congress Cataloging-in-Publication Data
Kipfer, Barbara Ann
      The wish list / by Barbara Ann Kipfer.
            p. cm.
      ISBN 0-7611-0756-8 (pbk.)
      1. Goal (psychology)—Miscellanea.
      2. Wishes—Miscellanea
      1. Title.
BF505.G6K57   1997
158.1—dc21   97-15092
                                  CIP

Workman books are available at special discounts when purchased in bulk for premiums and sales promotions as well as for fund-raising or educational use. Special editions for books excerpts can all be created to specification. For details, contact the Special Sales Director at the address below.

Workman Publishing Company
708 Broadway
New York, New York 10003-9555

Manufactured in the United States of America

First Printing October 1997
10 9 8 7 6 5 4 3 2

To Paul, Kyle, and Keir—you are my wish fulfilled. Thank you to Ruth Sullivan, Sally Kovalchick, and Peter Workman— believers once again!

INTRODUCTION

How many times have you started a sentence with the words "In my lifetime, I want to . . ."? Perhaps what you wanted was something grand, like winning a medal for bravery. Maybe it was something modest, even mundane—a wish to change jobs or to climb a tree. Maybe you wished for something fantastic—to be a country music star, for example. Or for something utterly practical, like making a budget and sticking to it. Your wish might have taken you to the other side of the world or as far away as the moon, or it might have meant just a walk around the corner. Maybe you wished to do something generous, or something just for you.

What happened to all those wishes? Where did they go?

Wishing is good for us. Daydreams, fantasies, castles in the air, and aspirations all drive us forward, impel us to make things happen. They also tell us a lot about ourselves. Our wishes come straight from our core, and they are loaded with vital information about who we are and who we can become. Keeping track of our wishes helps us tap into the energy that propels us to go after our happiness.

That's what *The Wish List* is for.

With close to 6,000 wishes, it is meant to serve as a wellspring of ideas for things to do, have, see, taste, experience, achieve, give, be, learn, do for others, or try—just once!—in this lifetime. Each item completes the sentence: "In my lifetime, I want to . . ." The collection ranges from small, easily realizable goals to grandiose pipe dreams—and everything in between. It works for ages 10 to 100. In fact, *The Wish List* looks a lot like your own hopes and dreams.

But I don't mean this list of wishes to be solely revelation. I mean it to be a useful tool—your own very personal "to do list for life." Carry *The Wish List* with you (it's highly portable) and when your creative daydreaming starts, scribble your own wishes on the blank lines. Check off or underline those wishes you want for yourself. When you've achieved a wish, celebrate the fact with a big red X in the box. As the years go by and *The Wish List*'s pages become dog-eared and yellow, you will have accumulated a profile of your changing view of happiness, your own evolving values, and your own fulfillments. Not a bad thing to have.

- ❏ try everything once
- ❏ win the Nobel Peace Prize
- ❏ play with the Chicago Bulls
- ❏ walk away with a hit movie and be catapulted from obscurity to stardom
- ❏ put an end to all civil and religious wars in the world
- ❏ have my "letter to the editor" published
- ❏ be elected President—in a landslide
- ❏ take off *now* for a spur-of-the-moment vacation
- ❏ design, build, and decorate my dream house
- ❏ clean-and-jerk three times my own weight
- ❏ scuba dive the Red Sea
- ❏ rehearse a Chekhov play with Vanessa Redgrave
- ❏ milk a cow
- ❏ load new software without having to call Tech Support
- ❏ ....
- ❏ ....

- ❑ bequeath enough money for my survivors to toast me with champagne each year on my birthday
- ❑ have cybersex—virtual, but very safe
- ❑ bodysurf off Malibu
- ❑ invent a holiday
- ❑ compose a perfect haiku
- ❑ not risk what I cannot afford to lose
- ❑ spend a romantic weekend in a luxury hotel on the French Riviera
- ❑ publish an article in a learned journal and see real scholars take it seriously
- ❑ walk down London's Abbey Road in homage to the Beatles
- ❑ sink a three-pointer in a basketball game
- ❑ ....
- ❑ ....
- ❑ ....
- ❑ learn sign language
- ❑ keep a stash of Girl Scout cookies all year round
- ❑ become a masseur

- ❏ spend a week kayaking among the islands on the coast of Maine
- ❏ volunteer at the Special Olympics
- ❏ write a best-selling, blockbuster bodice-ripper
- ❏ ....
- ❏ fly-fish the Yellowstone River
- ❏ spend the day noshing
- ❏ travel for three months with just one carry-on bag
- ❏ win a place on the U.S. Olympic team
- ❏ walk out of a dull, pointless meeting—just get up and walk out
- ❏ work for a company that has child care
- ❏ fall in love with the right person, at the right time for both of us
- ❏ trace the shape of a fossil from millions of years ago
- ❏ live closer to my family
- ❏ achieve more than is expected of me, faster, more efficiently, at less cost, for greater impact

- ❏ own a sensational sound system and have speakers in every room of the house
- ❏ look 30 at age 40, look 40 at age 50
- ❏ get an invention patented
- ❏ ....
- ❏ ....
- ❏ ....
- ❏ pass up the next chance to criticize
- ❏ wait out a storm in the bar of Windows on the World
- ❏ hike Alaska's Brooks Range
- ❏ attend a party on the terrace of a New York City penthouse
- ❏ be a doctor who makes house calls
- ❏ cast the next Hollywood blockbuster
- ❏ raise sheep
- ❏ give my lover a thousand Hershey's Kisses
- ❏ become a wine expert
- ❏ live in an all-electronic house I can control by computer
- ❏ adopt a baseball team of "hard-to-place" children

- ❑ solve a whole book of brainteasers
- ❑ scuba dive the wreck of a 16th-century Spanish galleon
- ❑ squeeze the Pillsbury Dough Boy just once to make him giggle
- ❑ take part in a geological survey
- ❑ keep exotic tropical fish
- ❑ join my neighbors in an impromptu Christmas caroling procession
- ❑ own a Rex, the only curly-haired cat
- ❑ reread all the original Nancy Drew mysteries
- ❑ attend the Grand Ole Opry
- ❑ get married in Notre Dame cathedral
- ❑ ....
- ❑ drive through a dust storm in the desert
- ❑ learn three jokes that get laughs every time
- ❑ run through Chicago's Buckingham fountain
- ❑ cook a perfect batch of popcorn for Paul Newman

- ❏ stop craving material things
- ❏ have enough space for my CDs
- ❏ celebrate Easter at St. Peter's in Rome
- ❏ bake croissants
- ❏ spend a summer in a chalet high in the Swiss Alps
- ❏ see a jazz funeral in New Orleans
- ❏ emcee the Grammys
- ❏ develop close friendships with people of different generations
- ❏ comprehend the Theory of Relativity
- ❏ own a collection of cacti and succulents
- ❏ ....
- ❏ ....
- ❏ ....
- ❏ ....
- ❏ build my own furniture
- ❏ make charcoal rubbings of the stones in a ghost town graveyard
- ❏ canoe the lakes of the Adirondacks
- ❏ learn to speed-read
- ❏ spend a day surfing the Internet

- ❏ take a botany vacation with renowned botanists
- ❏ ....
- ❏ ....
- ❏ ....
- ❏ own land on which there's a gravity-fed spring
- ❏ find inner peace
- ❏ volunteer as a school playground monitor
- ❏ get a walk-on part in my favorite soap opera
- ❏ throw a tailgate party for the homecoming game
- ❏ win the Pillsbury Bake-Off
- ❏ take the train into New Orleans across Lake Pontchartrain on the longest train bridge in the world
- ❏ study ballet for its discipline and drama
- ❏ win a week at Rancho la Puerta
- ❏ watch a cat give birth to a litter of kittens
- ❏ sell my crafts at a craft fair
- ❏ type 80 words a minute

- ❏ attend a testimonial dinner—as guest of honor
- ❏ work out for as much time each day as I spend eating
- ❏ ride a fire engine
- ❏ submit a suggestion that saves money for the company
- ❏ ....
- ❏ ....
- ❏ ....
- ❏ ....
- ❏ get a hit every time I step up to the plate
- ❏ receive an impassioned love letter
- ❏ finish paying off my college loans
- ❏ go to a sherry-tasting in Jerez, Spain, where sherry originated
- ❏ see a peregrine falcon in the wild
- ❏ score a perfect 10 in a gymnastics event
- ❏ be the first landowner on Mars
- ❏ spend a month in another century
- ❏ teach my dog to wipe his feet and shake off before he comes into the house

- ❑ swim in a pool on a cruise ship
- ❑ raise my IQ
- ❑ win the egg toss at the July 4 block party
- ❑ break the bank at Monte Carlo
- ❑ eat the world's best cheesecake at Junior's in Brooklyn
- ❑ drive I-80 from New York's George Washington Bridge to the Bay Bridge in San Francisco
- ❑ do the Sunday crossword puzzle in ink
- ❑ win the jackpot on a one-armed bandit in Las Vegas . . .
- ❑ . . . donate the jackpot to my alma mater
- ❑ ride the Moscow to St. Petersburg wide-gauge railroad
- ❑ see the gigantic carved heads of Easter Island
- ❑ stand on the shore and roar back at the ocean as loud as I can
- ❑ acknowledge my weaknesses
- ❑ have back-up singers echo me every time I say something important

- ❑ study Buddhist and Hindu dharma
- ❑ like Magellan, sight Tierra del Fuego
- ❑ be a mentor
- ❑ visit a new museum each month
- ❑ have tea with clotted cream in Devonshire, England
- ❑ go red-river rafting through the canyons of Mars
- ❑ play the course at Pebble Beach
- ❑ rent an entire restaurant for my 50th birthday party—preferably a restaurant in Paris
- ❑ end a meal with Stilton, fresh pears, and vintage Port
- ❑ concoct one great political cartoon
- ❑ ride a glider
- ❑ ....
- ❑ ....
- ❑ ....
- ❑ do pure science
- ❑ be a jazz disc jockey
- ❑ spin a plate on a stick

- ❑ live independently and magnanimously
- ❑ set a record in the sport I'm best at
- ❑ command a submarine so I can yell "Dive!
  Dive! Dive!"
- ❑ be there for a baby's first step
- ❑ ....
- ❑ ....
- ❑ ....
- ❑ ride a burro to the bottom of the Grand
  Canyon
- ❑ ride the bobsled course at Lillehammer
- ❑ read all of Proust
- ❑ leave my handprint on the sidewalk at
  Grauman's Chinese Theater
- ❑ join a *Messiah* sing-in at the Mormon
  Tabernacle
- ❑ attend my elementary school reunion
- ❑ hire a personal assistant
- ❑ throw the switch that lights up the
  national Christmas tree in Washington,
  D.C.
- ❑ overtip

- ❑ learn to tap dance
- ❑ drink tequila and lick salt from my hand on a beach in Mexico
- ❑ spend a day in the British Museum
- ❑ run off with the circus
- ❑ live to see the day when cash is electronic and I can buy the paper with my "currency card"
- ❑ set aside that grudge and bury the hatchet
- ❑ ....
- ❑ ....
- ❑ manage a great enterprise
- ❑ attend the Texas State Fair in Dallas, largest in the country
- ❑ save a half-year's salary
- ❑ build a better mousetrap
- ❑ sit through an opera by Wagner
- ❑ study philosophy
- ❑ give money and muscle to Habitat for Humanity
- ❑ umpire a major league game
- ❑ calculate with an abacus

- ❑ cook pasta that's perfectly al dente
- ❑ march in the Macy's Thanksgiving Day parade
- ❑ train the dog to play Frisbee
- ❑ visit a castle in Spain
- ❑ learn to repair my own car
- ❑ stay at the historic Mohonk Mountain House in New Paltz, New York
- ❑ earn an Eagle Scout badge
- ❑ play in a steel band in Trinidad
- ❑ go "undercover" and join a cult to see what it's like
- ❑ live without television
- ❑ mountain bike in the Rockies
- ❑ ....
- ❑ ....
- ❑ ....
- ❑ play the lead in a community theater production
- ❑ go behind the scenes at Disney World
- ❑ study the Tao to achieve effortless simplicity and freedom from desire

- ❑ surf cast for bass at Montauk Point
- ❑ break the sound barrier
- ❑ ....
- ❑ ....
- ❑ ....
- ❑ build a secret compartment into my desk
- ❑ live in a house designed by Frank Lloyd Wright
- ❑ spend an elegant weekend at the Gritti Palace hotel in Venice
- ❑ attend spring training
- ❑ make a killing in the stock market—then get out
- ❑ ride a helicopter to work
- ❑ slip into bed beside someone who's not expecting me
- ❑ ski Aspen
- ❑ serve regularly at the local soup kitchen
- ❑ bid at an auction
- ❑ write a letter to my descendants
- ❑ serve as the emcee of an evening's entertainment

- ❑ learn to read a river
- ❑ visit Windsor Castle
- ❑ wear only comfortable shoes
- ❑ write a sitcom based on the lives of my friends
- ❑ look great in Capri pants, mules, and a mohair twin set
- ❑ get through to *Car Talk* on National Public Radio so I can ask Click and Clack about that noise in the back end
- ❑ cruise the Greek Islands
- ❑ receive two dozen roses from an admirer
- ❑ ....
- ❑ ....
- ❑ trek the jungle of Borneo
- ❑ buy a lottery ticket for the one I love—and see it win
- ❑ start a watermelon garden
- ❑ attend the Calgary Stampede
- ❑ catch a foul ball and have the moment caught on television
- ❑ see with 20/20 vision

- ❏ float down the Amazon
- ❏ stop being judgmental
- ❏ live to see my children approve of my wardrobe
- ❏ ....
- ❏ ....
- ❏ ....
- ❏ use my time wisely
- ❏ tour the great sites of ancient Greece
- ❏ lie on the ground in a grove of giant sequoias, the largest living things on earth, and look up
- ❏ write a sonnet
- ❏ raise a barn
- ❏ walk across the Golden Gate Bridge
- ❏ live without envy
- ❏ ride an elephant in India
- ❏ see my alma mater win the NCAA basketball championship
- ❏ help preserve a landmark
- ❏ smell the freshness of the desert after a rain

- ☐ sail a sleek white yacht into the Bay of Naples at sunset
- ☐ find my great love late in life
- ☐ fly over "the roof of the world"—the 96 Himalayan peaks, reaching over 24,000 feet high
- ☐ see the New York Jets win the Super Bowl again
- ☐ set aside time each day to be totally alone
- ☐ hire an organization expert, follow her advice, then stick to it
- ☐ see where the Hatfields feuded with the McCoys
- ☐ learn to box
- ☐ break a mirror and not worry

- ☐ receive an invitation to Buckingham Palace
- ☐ ....
- ☐ ....
- ☐ surf the big waves off Australia's west coast
- ☐ find a genuine arrowhead

- ❑ summer in a villa in Tuscany
- ❑ schedule one day a week for creative thinking—all day
- ❑ win a speaking role in a movie
- ❑ be featured, benignly, in *Doonesbury*
- ❑ ski the Olympic jump at Squaw Valley
- ❑ earn a raise for my people-management skills
- ❑ with the *Odyssey* as my travel guide, retrace Ulysses' route home
- ❑ throw out the first ball on opening day
- ❑ drive a Maserati
- ❑ lasso a steer from horseback
- ❑ eat Doritos and Oreos without guilt
- ❑ trek in Nepal
- ❑ write a great headline
- ❑ ....
- ❑ ....
- ❑ force hyacinths to bloom from bulbs
- ❑ bike the Greenbrier River Trail in West Virginia
- ❑ discover a cure for cancer

❑ understand all the layers of *King Lear*

❑ win a medal for bravery

❑ ....

❑ ....

❑ ....

❑ canoe the Allagash in Maine

❑ cook a perfect omelet

❑ determine what is the one thing in life I
   want most

❑ become a tree surgeon

❑ dance a Viennese waltz in Vienna

❑ get a tattoo

❑ go on a walking tour of the Loire Valley

❑ skydive

❑ celebrate my birthday aboard a yacht in
   the Mediterranean

❑ own a pair of Bollé wraparound sunglasses

❑ learn to Roller Blade

❑ host an inner-city kid at the beach
   for the summer

❑ become a logger in the Northwest

❑ stop a mugger

- ❏ skinny-dip under a waterfall
- ❏ celebrate St. Patrick's Day in Dublin
- ❏ ....
- ❏ ....
- ❏ ....
- ❏ ....
- ❏ throw a party people will talk about for
  years
- ❏ achieve the peacock-in-lotus yoga pose
- ❏ win an Oscar
- ❏ dine in a five-star restaurant in France
- ❏ take my family on a backpacking trip
  through the Grand Tetons
- ❏ observe an avalanche (from a safe
  distance)
- ❏ be a world-famous fashion designer
- ❏ shake hands with Willie Mays
- ❏ attend the Iowa caucuses
- ❏ crack a secret code
- ❏ travel to Bali to hear gamelan music on its
  native ground
- ❏ experience an epiphany

❑ start a patchwork quilt on the day of my
child's birth—and give her the finished
product on the day she
graduates from college
❑ beat the Guinness world
record for skipping stones
❑ stick to my convictions even in the face of
hostile opposition
❑ walk on stilts
❑ take a boat ride through Indiana's
Wyandotte Cave
❑ start a reading group
❑ finish everything I set out to do
❑ see where the red salmon spawn on Lake
Clark in Alaska
❑ ....
❑ ....
❑ be asked for the recipe for something
I've cooked
❑ pamper myself with "the works" at a
luxury spa
❑ take a limo to a Broadway opening

- ❑ do a laughing meditation
- ❑ trek through Karakoram
- ❑ attain my official "ideal weight"
- ❑ play the Augusta National Golf Club course, scene of the Masters
- ❑ whittle a child's toy
- ❑ choose how to live the last year of my life
- ❑ travel the coast of Turkey
- ❑ take a kid to the circus
- ❑ ....
- ❑ ....
- ❑ ....
- ❑ burn my bridges
- ❑ visit Valley Forge in a winter as severe as that of 1777–78
- ❑ get a cosmetic makeover
- ❑ tell those I love how much I appreciate them
- ❑ make the cover of *Time* magazine
- ❑ revisit my childhood home with my siblings
- ❑ cut my own firewood with a chain saw

- ❏ cross the Cumberland Gap of the Appalachian Mountains, following Daniel Boone's Wilderness Road to the Old West
- ❏ drive a four-wheeler up a mountain
- ❏ ....
- ❏ ....
- ❏ ....
- ❏ play in a bell choir
- ❏ pull a drowning person to safety—even one who's drowning in despair
- ❏ avoid the symptoms of menopause
- ❏ dig a pond on my property and stock it with fish
- ❏ celebrate Mardi Gras in New Orleans
- ❏ log on to an encyclopedia that's updated daily
- ❏ have a shipboard romance
- ❏ race a car at Watkins Glen
- ❏ be invited backstage by Pavarotti
- ❏ own a portable global positioning system and never get lost
- ❏ nurse a sick animal back to health

- ☐ snowmobile in Finland
- ☐ make love in a public place
- ☐ make my own pickles
- ☐ kayak over the Grand Canyon's Lava Falls

- ☐ write a speech for the President
- ☐ take a woodworking class
- ☐ receive a phone call out of the blue from a headhunter
- ☐ travel back through time to the glory that was Greece and the grandeur that was Rome
- ☐ vote in every election for which I'm eligible
- ☐ be granted an audience with the Pope
- ☐ ....
- ☐ ....
- ☐ ....
- ☐ commit to something totally
- ☐ lunch at New York's "21"
- ☐ split logs with sledgehammer and wedge
- ☐ sit in the Royal Box at London's Covent Garden theater

- ❏ paint a sidewalk mosaic
- ❏ spend five days focusing on each of my five senses—one day per sense
- ❏ ....
- ❏ ....
- ❏ get elected team captain
- ❏ move into a new house but wait a month before bringing in furniture
- ❏ run my own business
- ❏ learn and use a new word each day
- ❏ study at the Short Game Golf School at the Boca Raton Resort and Club
- ❏ teach high school and inspire at least one kid to love poetry
- ❏ discover a sibling I didn't know I had
- ❏ improve my grammar
- ❏ create a computer database for my family tree
- ❏ pay off my credit cards
- ❏ sit in the infield for the Indianapolis 500
- ❏ visit the restored buildings of Colonial Williamsburg

- ❑ drink chilled Manzanilla accompanied by olives and almonds
- ❑ hit the road for a year in an RV
- ❑ go three for three from the free-throw line
- ❑ stick to an exercise regimen—for the rest of my life
- ❑ direct a music video starring Sting
- ❑ live and work in Beijing for a year
- ❑ mind my own business
- ❑ spend a day watching the sun move across the sky
- ❑ live in a villa on the Italian Riviera
- ❑ operate a Ouija board
- ❑ be the sole holdout on a jury—and hang it if I must
- ❑ mud slide in the rain
- ❑ do spring cleaning *before* Memorial Day
- ❑ watch a bud open
- ❑ see summer arrive in Antarctica
- ❑ visit Louisiana's Oak Alley plantation to imagine antebellum life
- ❑ keep in touch with far-flung relatives

- ❏ invent a replacement for dental floss
- ❏ take charge of my own contentment
- ❏ explore West Africa
- ❏ bake scones
- ❏ take a battery of tests to identify my strengths and weaknesses
- ❏ work in flextime so I can balance career and family
- ❏ ....
- ❏ ....
- ❏ ....
- ❏ ....
- ❏ own a set of Limoges china
- ❏ visit Utah's Bryce Canyon
- ❏ store snowballs in the freezer and pull them out for a summer party
- ❏ avoid baldness
- ❏ bowl a perfect game in the league championship
- ❏ get in touch with a former life
- ❏ put a compass in my car so I know I'm headed in the right direction

- ❏ overcome difficulties in a relationship
- ❏ write a children's book in which the protagonist is a character very like my own child
- ❏ redecorate my home from top to bottom
- ❏ create a secret code
- ❏ walk the fabled Bund in Shanghai
- ❏ discover a lost Shakespeare sonnet
- ❏ make my own maple syrup
- ❏ spend a weekend in Atlantic City
- ❏ avoid clichés
- ❏ run an antiques shop
- ❏ see Haleakala Crater on Maui
- ❏ invent an alternative to panty hose and tights
- ❏ enjoy fresh tomatoes in December
- ❏ stand at the foot of K-2 in the Karakoram Mountains of northern India, the world's second-highest peak
- ❏ create a best-selling detective character
- ❏ have lunch with my best friend from elementary school

- ❏ need only five hours of sleep
- ❏ visit the National Aviation Hall of Fame in
    Dayton, Ohio
- ❏ dine with Vaclav Havel
- ❏ sleep till noon every day for a week
- ❏ spend a stormy night in a
    lighthouse on a rocky coast
- ❏ grow championship dahlias
- ❏ visit every one of the national parks
- ❏ drive one of the big rigs, an 18-wheeler, flat
    out on the interstate
- ❏ make all my own clothes
- ❏ dog-sled across Alaska
- ❏ be in goal for one period in a professional
    hockey game
- ❏ ....
- ❏ ....
- ❏ ....
- ❏ ....
- ❏ sleep in a stable surrounded by animals
- ❏ find a love letter from my great-grandfather
    to my great-grandmother

❑ start every new year with a clean house, an
    uncluttered desk, and a new date book

❑ motorcycle across Nevada's desert flats

❑ be a five-time *Jeopardy* winner

❑ live to see a room, building, or park named
    for me

❑ spend a summer and fall eating only what
    I've grown in my own garden

❑ learn to draw

❑ observe an American bald eagle in the wild

❑ build a room of my own

❑ eat Oregon apple pie in Portland, then
    drive north for Washington peach pie in
    Seattle

❑ be able to help my teenage son with his
    homework

❑ sing in a barbershop quartet

❑ get a floor pass to a national political
    convention

❑ ....

❑ ....

❑ overcome my shyness

- ❏ take a bubble bath in Raffles Hotel in Singapore
- ❏ have an astrologer cast my chart
- ❏ work the phones at a charity telethon
- ❏ travel with a sports team for a season and write a book about it
- ❏ ....
- ❏ ....
- ❏ study cooking at Le Cordon Bleu in Paris
- ❏ swim with the grace of a stingray
- ❏ build a harpsichord from a kit
- ❏ learn Arabic so I can write its beautiful alphabet
- ❏ canoe the Boundary Waters
- ❏ assist at the birth of a foal
- ❏ hear zydeco music in the bayou country
- ❏ come home to find dinner ready on the table
- ❏ hug a redwood
- ❏ visit Ouagadougou, capital of Burkina Faso in West Africa
- ❏ look good without makeup

❑ shop along Rodeo Drive

❑ confront anxiety with grace and humor

❑ program my VCR with ease

❑ know what my baby is thinking

❑ ride horseback through Ireland

❑ ....

❑ ....

❑ ....

❑ eliminate roaches and rats forever

❑ travel with no destination

❑ hear Jessye Norman sing, live and in
   person

❑ spend a night on the town with Harrison
   Ford

❑ ride out a hurricane on North Carolina's
   Outer Banks

❑ learn to meditate so I can center my mind
   and calm my spirit

❑ taste raw sugarcane on a Caribbean island

❑ be part of a human pyramid—preferably,
   the apex

❑ host my own weekly radio program

- ❑ hit a curveball thrown by a major-league pitcher, then hit his fastball
- ❑ not just meet but exceed the expectations of the people I love
- ❑ learn to rock-climb
- ❑ see a moose in the wild—a full-grown male with a handsome rack of antlers
- ❑ watch a ballet from the wings of the theater
- ❑ bicycle across my home state, and if I like it well enough . . .
- ❑ . . . bicycle across the country
- ❑ see the cacti bloom in the Mojave Desert
- ❑ be chosen by a beauty magazine as its makeover candidate
- ❑ write a book that changes someone's life for the better
- ❑ ....
- ❑ ....
- ❑ sail the inland waterway down the Eastern Seaboard
- ❑ make the shot that wins the game just as the final buzzer sounds

- ❏ give away everything I haven't worn in three years
- ❏ take a pack trip on horseback through Yellowstone National Park
- ❏ feel wistful but not gloomy about the past
- ❏ talk a friend into the hairdo I've always thought she should have
- ❏ ....
- ❏ ....
- ❏ ....
- ❏ ....
- ❏ learn to speak French
- ❏ spend a day as a citizen of Pompeii
- ❏ find the best truck stop in Montana
- ❏ get so good at poker I really know when to hold 'em and when to fold 'em
- ❏ make and keep a commitment to a cause I believe in
- ❏ shop at the 24-hour L.L. Bean store in Freeport, Maine, at 3:00 in the morning
- ❏ move into the corner office with a view
- ❏ make a perfect soufflé

- ❑ sing with a band in a nightclub
- ❑ ....
- ❑ ....
- ❑ eat a meal cooked by Julia Child
- ❑ snorkel Australia's Great Barrier Reef
- ❑ learn to tie a perfect bowline knot
- ❑ be a spear-carrier in an opera
- ❑ hold an audience spellbound
- ❑ own a bright red, soft-leather La-Z-Boy chair
- ❑ study Brunelleschi's system for drawing in perspective
- ❑ watch the sun set over Machu Picchu
- ❑ gather the neighbors and plant a community garden
- ❑ work as a taster at Ben & Jerry's
- ❑ get something off my chest in an Op-Ed piece and see it published
- ❑ get the amaryllis on my windowsill to bloom in winter
- ❑ master the Internet
- ❑ organize a filing system that works
- ❑ take a course in sculpture

- ❏ enjoy having a willowy figure and long, straight hair—at least for a month or so
- ❏ learn to express myself colorfully without using profanity
- ❏ relive the last week before high school graduation
- ❏ ....
- ❏ ....
- ❏ ....
- ❏ swim with dolphins
- ❏ finish my dissertation
- ❏ on a long airplane ride, sit next to someone who *really* does not want to talk
- ❏ watch the lava flowing out of Kilauea
- ❏ grow my own flax, then twist it into rope and weave it into cloth
- ❏ pay off my mortgage and throw a party to celebrate
- ❏ go from London to Paris via the Chunnel
- ❏ sit for my portrait
- ❏ collect enough individual ceramic tiles to cover one wall of my kitchen

- ❏ explore the caves of Lascaux and their 20,000-year-old wall paintings
- ❏ ....
- ❏ ....
- ❏ visit the country my spouse's family came from—and look for cultural clues
- ❏ climb Mount McKinley, reaching the summit just as day breaks
- ❏ cross-dress for a day
- ❏ own a big-screen televison
- ❏ drink sherry and eat tapas in Spain
- ❏ see a grizzly bear in the wild from a safe distance
- ❏ really spend a vacation lying on a beach reading all the books I've been saving up
- ❏ fly the Concorde
- ❏ go on safari across Africa's Serengeti Plain
- ❏ work for a person I've always admired
- ❏ see a great white shark
- ❏ pass a wilderness survival test
- ❏ create a bonsai forest

- ❏ ride bareback along a beach at sunrise
- ❏ vacation on a Pacific island you can only get to by sailboat
- ❏ count my blessings
- ❏ be willing to risk my self-image
- ❏ eat street food in Bangkok and wash it down with ice-cold Thai beer
- ❏ stay overnight at the White House
- ❏ own a Louis Vuitton steamer trunk
- ❏ gain the one ability that has always eluded me
- ❏ ride the train down the Malaysian peninsula from Bangleole to Kuala Lumpur
- ❏ ....
- ❏ ....
- ❏ ....
- ❏ take a trip to Disney World when no one else is there
- ❏ journey along the Silk Road from China to the Mediterranean
- ❏ have a lush lawn with neither crabgrass nor weeds

- ❑ own a Ming vase
- ❑ ....
- ❑ ....
- ❑ climb the Great Pyramid at Giza
- ❑ throw caution to the wind and see a movie *before* it's reviewed
- ❑ spend a day on a nude beach
- ❑ design a coffee table for people (like me) who like to use it as a footstool
- ❑ work at an employee-owned company
- ❑ become a Big Brother or Big Sister to a child who needs one
- ❑ be a supermodel
- ❑ see a meteor crater
- ❑ bird-watch for sandhill cranes along the Platte River in Nebraska
- ❑ play in a symphony orchestra
- ❑ marry for money, then fall in love
- ❑ cut my commuting time in half
- ❑ stand in the center of the Roman Colosseum
- ❑ mow a putting green

- ❑ find an extra $1,000 in my bank account
- ❑ ride aboard the Goodyear blimp
- ❑ have lunch in the restaurant atop Seattle's Space Needle
- ❑ swing on a trapeze
- ❑ share a small tent in the wilderness with the one I love
- ❑ prepare a salad using 20 different ingredients
- ❑ think up a bumper sticker slogan and see it on cars driving by
- ❑ negotiate a contract
- ❑ visit Antarctica to see the emperor penguins
- ❑ ....
- ❑ ....
- ❑ declare every day "dress down Friday"
- ❑ write the lyrics to a hit song that people can't stop singing
- ❑ own a cashmere coat
- ❑ swing on a trapeze
- ❑ learn something new every day

❑ peer over the lip of an active volcano

❑ ....

❑ ....

❑ ....

❑ read the complete works of Shakespeare

❑ get a bad law changed

❑ arrive punctually for every appointment

❑ winter on a dude ranch in New Mexico,
    then . . .

❑ . . . summer on a dude ranch in Wyoming

❑ learn to read music

❑ visit the Taj Mahal, monument to love, with
    the person I love

❑ train my dog to perfect obedience

❑ see the Acropolis of Athens in the
    moonlight

❑ help the sea turtles on Big Island, Hawaii,
    back into the sea after they've
    been hatched

❑ take an entire summer off from work

❑ work out in a private, personal
    exercise room

- ❑ ride the Chihuahua-Pacifico railroad through Mexico's spectacular Copper Canyon country
- ❑ live in a house with all Shaker furniture
- ❑ ....
- ❑ ....
- ❑ nap in a field of wildflowers
- ❑ spend a rainy Saturday listening to opera on the radio
- ❑ land on water in a seaplane
- ❑ raise my standard of living
- ❑ travel to Tibet, where pilgrims prostrate themselves each step of the way to the holy city of Lhasa
- ❑ live next door to a concert pianist
- ❑ create a fragrance and name it after myself
- ❑ learn how to rewire a lamp
- ❑ remember to stop and smell the roses
- ❑ visit George Washington's home at Mount Vernon
- ❑ be a country music star
- ❑ do a flying camel on ice skates

- ❑ hike among the Berber villages of Morocco's Atlas Mountains
- ❑ float on the Great Salt Lake
- ❑ see the statue of Edgar Allan Poe in the Bronx, New York
- ❑ fly first class around the world on Cathay Pacific
- ❑ walk a dog for a sick neighbor
- ❑ paint a mural on Cleveland's Terminal Tower
- ❑ weave a wreath of frangipani flowers in Hawaii
- ❑ tour the ruins of the "rose-red city" of Petra, Jordan, on horseback
- ❑ smell the crisp pages of a new book
- ❑ ....
- ❑ ....
- ❑ be named ambassador to Barbados
- ❑ own the latest generation of computer equipment
- ❑ go back in time to party with Scott and Zelda Fitzgerald

- ❏ ....
- ❏ do nothing all day and feel no guilt
- ❏ compete as a sprinter in the Millrose Games at Madison Square Garden
- ❏ attend the jazz festivals at Newport, Monterey, and Sacramento
- ❏ own a sport-utility vehicle that does not guzzle gas
- ❏ send flowers to the one I love for no reason at all
- ❏ bike the roads of the Swiss Alps
- ❏ experiment with life, mixing ingredients and trying new formulas
- ❏ star in a Broadway play
- ❏ collect pewter
- ❏ play Santa Claus at a Christmas party for underprivileged children
- ❏ spend a week in a hotel on the Ile St. Louis in Paris
- ❏ visit all the Union Stations in the country
- ❏ eat fried zucchini blossoms in Rome as soon as they're in season

- ❏ spend a week doing no housework and no yard work
- ❏ attend the Shakespeare Festival in Ashland, Oregon
- ❏ own a plain-paper fax machine
- ❏ drive across Kansas when the wheat is ready for harvest
- ❏ grind my own coffee beans for my morning cup
- ❏ keep my watch on 24-hour "military" time
- ❏ grow next year's garlic from this year's cloves
- ❏ spend Bastille Day in Paris
- ❏ have a really honest conversation with my parents
- ❏ have a really honest conversation with my children
- ❏ ....
- ❏ ....
- ❏ ....
- ❏ ....

- ❑ decipher the language of the ancient Etruscans
- ❑ raft the big bend of the Rio Grande
- ❑ race at Daytona
- ❑ sleep in a hammock above the rain forest
- ❑ find a cure for the common cold
- ❑ take over for the ailing star and win raves
- ❑ become a late bloomer
- ❑ wake up without an alarm clock
- ❑ ....
- ❑ ....
- ❑ ....
- ❑ read *War and Peace* in Russian
- ❑ go for a moonlight sail around San Francisco Bay
- ❑ visit every major league baseball stadium
- ❑ write a perfect short story that's selected for inclusion in an anthology
- ❑ invent bifocal contact lenses that work
- ❑ spend the whole summer camping out
- ❑ be friends with a mad genius
- ❑ join a string quartet

❑ lead my hometown's Fourth of July parade
❑ understand exactly how a car works
❑ ....
❑ ....
❑ call the White House and have the
   President answer
❑ study Aristotle's philosophy
❑ help an amateur athlete realize his/her
   professional potential
❑ be asked to model high fashion
❑ whistle with two fingers in my mouth
❑ create a happy family life
❑ make a dress that's a copy of the one my
   Barbie doll had
❑ escape to a cabin in the New Hampshire
   woods for a month of rest and restoration
❑ be a guest observer at the next launch of
   the space shuttle
❑ stop trying to control the uncontrollable
❑ abolish car alarms
❑ make love on a bearskin rug in front of
   a roaring fire

- ❑ ....
- ❑ ....
- ❑ challenge "Deep Blue" at chess
- ❑ get bumped up to first class and find myself next to my favorite movie star
- ❑ learn to cut stone
- ❑ ride a thousand-dollar bicycle
- ❑ dribble a basketball like Meadowlark Lemon
- ❑ go on sabbatical
- ❑ see the large, doughnut-like stones that are the ancient money of Yap in Micronesia
- ❑ try sushi
- ❑ accept that pain and disappointment are part of life
- ❑ attain the next belt in tae kwon do
- ❑ paint the sets for a show
- ❑ learn how to juggle
- ❑ find a pearl in an oyster
- ❑ concentrate on everything I do
- ❑ sit courtside at a Knicks-Bulls game

- ❑ crack open a geode
- ❑ understand cricket, and try to understand cricket madness
- ❑ eat less meat
- ❑ do the calligraphy for my own wedding invitation
- ❑ install an indoor lap pool in the basement
- ❑ sing a solo at the church Christmas concert
- ❑ make a "living fence" of ocotillo cactus
- ❑ work in a company that gives bonuses
- ❑ rediscover old friends
- ❑ take a New Age escape in Sedona, Arizona
- ❑ not eat all I can eat at an all-you-can-eat restaurant
- ❑ ....
- ❑ ....
- ❑ ....
- ❑ keep notebooks in every room of the house so I can jot down thoughts on the spot
- ❑ learn Italian

- ❑ change careers in mid-life
- ❑ go whitewater rafting in Costa Rica
- ❑ sing in a Gilbert and Sullivan operetta
- ❑ design a bridge
- ❑ present the Oscar for Best Picture
- ❑ go on a "zoo tour" of the world
- ❑ invest in art
- ❑ measure up to my own expectations for myself
- ❑ understand quantum mechanics
- ❑ spend every February in a different warm destination
- ❑ ....
- ❑ ....
- ❑ ....
- ❑ ....
- ❑ volunteer at a hospital
- ❑ pilot an airplane through a barrel roll
- ❑ build up my strengths
- ❑ diminish my weaknesses
- ❑ remember my dreams and try to construe their meaning

- ❑ go around the world in 80 days
- ❑ experience a mild earth tremor
- ❑ ....
- ❑ ....
- ❑ meet the Librarian of Congress
- ❑ attend the Triple Crown—the Kentucky Derby, Preakness, and Belmont Stakes
- ❑ sit in on a jam session with the Marsalis family
- ❑ dress for me, not for a fashion trend
- ❑ touch a whale
- ❑ ski well enough to join the ski patrol
- ❑ seek harmony
- ❑ attend a party hosted by Dennis Rodman
- ❑ ride in a steeplechase
- ❑ spend the night locked in the Chicago Art Institute
- ❑ gain the knack of reading upside down
- ❑ climb the dome of the Duomo in Florence, Italy
- ❑ get a poem accepted by *The New Yorker*
- ❑ learn carpentry

❑ know what I can overlook
❑ wake up a half hour earlier and take a walk
❑ earn a million dollars
❑ be able to do one great impression of a
   celebrity
❑ ....
❑ ....
❑ ....
❑ visit the National Archives and examine
   the actual Declaration of Independence
   and the Constitution
❑ in-line skate the boardwalk on the New
   Jersey shore
❑ design a children's playground with a
   group of children
❑ consider the alternative
❑ drive a bulldozer for a day
❑ accept that it's okay to be me
❑ learn the art of origami
❑ watch less television and better television
❑ diagram the Gettysburg Address so I can
   see Lincoln's logic at work

- ❑ play steel drums
- ❑ capture a great moment on camera
- ❑ earn a cool nickname
- ❑ travel abroad for a year
- ❑ add a screened sleeping porch to my house and sleep there all summer long
- ❑ master Rachmaninoff's Third Piano Concerto
- ❑ learn the constellations—once and for all
- ❑ work at a stand-up desk
- ❑ create rather than complain
- ❑ find a four-leaf clover
- ❑ construct an ice sculpture
- ❑ make sure *I* make the choices that shape my life
- ❑ talk someone out of commiting a crime
- ❑ ....
- ❑ ....
- ❑ study the Dialogues of Plato
- ❑ praise rather than criticize
- ❑ walk across Europe from the North Sea to the Mediterranean

❑ acquire the ability to speak articulately "off the cuff" in public

❑ ....

❑ ....

❑ play a love scene with Robert Redford

❑ attend the Inaugural Ball

❑ produce a popular comic strip

❑ visit the nation's oldest botanical garden, founded by John Bartram in Pennsylvania in 1728

❑ see my children happily married

❑ donate to a sperm bank

❑ appear on a late-night talk show

❑ inherit a vacation home on the Maine coast

❑ be the first to fight for a just cause

❑ reread my favorite book

❑ own a remote car-radio disabler

❑ have a passionate affair in a bougainvillea-covered villa on the island of Capri

❑ paint a portrait

❑ become the gossip columnist for the local paper

- ❏ travel to outer space
- ❏ skipper a Mississippi riverboat from Wisconsin to the Gulf
- ❏ win a game of Trivial Pursuit
- ❏ ride in a rodeo
- ❏ cut down my own Christmas tree
- ❏ stand on the equator
- ❏ paint my house inside and out
- ❏ ride the switchback train out of Kamloops, British Columbia
- ❏ complete college in three years
- ❏ drive a vintage Corvette
- ❏ ....
- ❏ ....
- ❏ ....
- ❏ ....
- ❏ serve my country
- ❏ see my home featured in *Architectural Digest*
- ❏ accept my life for what it is—and embrace it
- ❏ climb the Matterhorn

- ❑ design the costumes for a Broadway musical
- ❑ see the sun rise in Kiribati, where the day begins
- ❑ follow the route the wagon trains took along the Oregon Trail, from the Missouri River to the Willamette Valley
- ❑ taste a century-old wine
- ❑ ....
- ❑ read Virgil's *Aeneid* in the original Latin
- ❑ learn to listen, not just to hear
- ❑ visit the land of my ancestors
- ❑ wiggle my ears to make a baby laugh
- ❑ see my writing praised by a Pulitzer Prize–winning author
- ❑ fish and hike in the Ozarks
- ❑ receive an anonymous gift and never learn who it's from
- ❑ travel overseas on a diplomatic mission
- ❑ take up yoga
- ❑ move to the place where I've always wanted to live

- [ ] watch the pelicans in San Francisco Bay
- [ ] ....
- [ ] ....
- [ ] ....
- [ ] surprise an old friend with a phone call
- [ ] dare to play Truth or Dare
- [ ] become a good debater
- [ ] design jewelry
- [ ] keep bees and make honey
- [ ] write a first novel at the age of 80
- [ ] discover the lost island of Atlantis
- [ ] drive a Porsche
- [ ] learn to bend under stress, not submit to it
- [ ] do stand-up comedy
- [ ] tour what was once the Utopian
  community of New Harmony, Indiana
- [ ] wear a sari with grace
- [ ] make love under mosquito netting
- [ ] grow a rose garden
- [ ] watch a center-court match at Wimbledon
- [ ] discover a preventive for AIDS
- [ ] cruise the Nile in a felucca

- ❑ take one long and two short vacations every year
- ❑ win a spelling bee
- ❑ explore the farthest, coldest reaches of the Arctic
- ❑ equip my car with compact-disk player, tape deck, and super speakers
- ❑ levitate
- ❑ shoot three under par on the golf course
- ❑ ride through Central Park in a horse-drawn carriage
- ❑ see a panda in the wild
- ❑ sit in on classes in my old high school—just to see if I've learned anything since
- ❑ ....
- ❑ ....
- ❑ ....
- ❑ be able to repair household plumbing and electrical fixtures myself
- ❑ cuddle a lion cub
- ❑ see the Cathedral of Autun, France
- ❑ spend the summer at a writers' colony

- ❑ take the family on a cross-country camping trip through the National Parks
- ❑ ....
- ❑ ....
- ❑ add bird of paradise to my bird-watching life list
- ❑ in Italy, eat at a ristorante, a trattoria, a pizzeria, a pasticceria, and a gelateria—all in one day
- ❑ donate my library to the library
- ❑ make the finals in a dance marathon
- ❑ drink Napoleon brandy
- ❑ join an archaeological dig and uncover something long buried
- ❑ understand taxation well enough to debate it
- ❑ learn to love cereal without sugar, sandwiches without mayo, salad without olive oil
- ❑ identify my mission in life
- ❑ win a one-month trip to the destination of my choice

- ❑ dream in color
- ❑ be the wind beneath someone else's wings
- ❑ pilot a helicopter
- ❑ volunteer time at an animal shelter
- ❑ watch *Sesame Street* with my grandchildren
- ❑ own a fire-engine-red convertible
- ❑ throw a dinner party for 20—effortlessly
- ❑ train for the triathlon
- ❑ look good with my head shaved
- ❑ see a bullfight in Valladolid, Spain
- ❑ take apart a telephone and put it back together
- ❑ invent bug-resistant lettuce
- ❑ ....
- ❑ ....
- ❑ ....
- ❑ ....
- ❑ frame a picture
- ❑ join an investment club and invest only in companies that do not pollute
- ❑ become a rock star

❑ receive a letter from Mother Theresa
❑ eat fresh corn on the cob in January
❑ work on a political campaign
❑ learn to sail
❑ remember all the words
   to my favorite songs

❑ make love in the ocean
❑ live in such a way that my behavior
   causes no embarrassment to
   anyone—especially me
❑ own an old-fashioned jukebox
❑ attend the Venice Biennale art exhibit
❑ join in the "wave" at the ballpark
❑ browse through the 22 volumes of the *Oxford
   English Dictionary,* just for fun
❑ study the biographies of the ten people I
   most admire
❑ see fields of red poppies in the south of
   France
❑ have a fireplace in my bedroom
❑ send my mother-in-law flowers on my
   spouse's birthday

- ❏ build a sailboat
- ❏ harvest wheat in Kansas
- ❏ motorcycle through Glacier National Park
- ❏ ....
- ❏ ....
- ❏ ....
- ❏ make my own tequila from my own agave
- ❏ make a close friend late in life
- ❏ discover a lost manuscript of ancient Latin poetry
- ❏ not be embarrassed to make a fool of myself
- ❏ snuggle under a goosedown quilt in the middle of winter
- ❏ sing all the old camp songs
- ❏ see my team win the Stanley Cup
- ❏ see puffins in the wild
- ❏ give my house the white-glove test—and have it pass!
- ❏ open a microbrewery
- ❏ be able to nap for 10 minutes and wake up refreshed

- ❑ reach down for reserves of inner strength—
  and find them
- ❑ read every book I own
- ❑ fly over the Na Pali coast of Maui in a
  helicopter
- ❑ beat my personal best
- ❑ carry out just one of my many "million-
  dollar" ideas
- ❑ be the first to spot trillium in the spring
- ❑ become an organic farmer
- ❑ meet a Beatle
- ❑ use homemade toothpaste
- ❑ see the Northern Lights in Sweden
- ❑ savor life's joys
- ❑ study art with my favorite artist
- ❑ ride with the engineer and help drive the
  train
- ❑ buy an entire secondhand wardrobe
- ❑ fish for wild trout in Scotland
- ❑ ....
- ❑ ....
- ❑ ....

- ❏ earn six weeks' paid vacation
- ❏ design a greeting card that becomes a Hallmark classic
- ❏ ride the Cyclone at Coney Island
- ❏ find an oasis in the desert
- ❏ marry in a candlelight ceremony
- ❏ become a middle school teacher—getting kids at their most curious
- ❏ walk on a moving sidewalk
- ❏ stand up for my principles— even if I stand alone
- ❏ ride a hot-air balloon over the Arizona desert
- ❏ ....
- ❏ ....
- ❏ catch a marlin
- ❏ become a renowned surgeon
- ❏ rub two sticks together and start a fire
- ❏ grill fresh salmon on a hibachi
- ❏ walk across the bridges over the Seine in Paris
- ❏ draw outside the lines

- ❑ do karaoke
- ❑ visit all of the 50 states
- ❑ lead a successful boycott of produce from farms hiring non-union farm workers
- ❑ taste blood pudding
- ❑ ride in the caboose
- ❑ ....
- ❑ ....
- ❑ ....
- ❑ dance all night
- ❑ participate in a professional magic trick
- ❑ grow all my own herbs
- ❑ Rollerblade down the spiraling ramp of the Guggenheim Museum
- ❑ give anonymously to charity
- ❑ visit Graceland
- ❑ read the complete works of Jane Austen
- ❑ dance like Michael Flatley
- ❑ lay a tile floor
- ❑ have Martha Stewart ask me for a recipe
- ❑ ride the Orient Express
- ❑ perform in *Hello, Dolly*

- ❑ make a difference in the life of someone I care about
- ❑ find inspiration in a work of art
- ❑ paddle the Tippecanoe River in Indiana
- ❑ sit in on a recording session with Barbra Streisand
- ❑ slide down a really long banister
- ❑ get through the *Encyclopaedia Britannica* from A to Z
- ❑ spot my house from an airplane
- ❑ write a play
- ❑ make homemade ice cream
- ❑ ....
- ❑ ....
- ❑ ....
- ❑ negotiate a big deal involving lots of participants and gobs of money
- ❑ run a race at the site of the first Olympics
- ❑ spend a hot day on a lawn chair under the sprinkler
- ❑ spend a vacation volunteering at a camp for kids with cancer

- ❏ dream consistently pleasant dreams
- ❏ climb Alaska's Chilkoot Pass
- ❏ have a one-night stand with my childhood sweetheart
- ❏ ....
- ❏ ....
- ❏ hang glide over the Cascade Mountains
- ❏ make real piecrust from scratch
- ❏ build a log cabin from a kit
- ❏ become a jazz singer
- ❏ attend the yearly sale at Harrod's department store in London
- ❏ drive a stagecoach
- ❏ manage a baseball team
- ❏ take a Greyhound bus across the country
- ❏ retire at age 50
- ❏ be photogenic
- ❏ persuade Congress to strengthen the national commitment to the arts
- ❏ cross-country ski down the middle of Chicago's Loop
- ❏ pipe laments on a Scottish bagpipe

- ❑ invent a floor surface that never needs cleaning
- ❑ study comparative religion
- ❑ become a landscape architect
- ❑ ....
- ❑ ....
- ❑ bind my cherished books in leather and edge the pages in gold
- ❑ take up interval training
- ❑ renovate a Victorian farmhouse
- ❑ drive Virginia's Blue Ridge Parkway in spring when the azaleas are in bloom
- ❑ have a private viewing of the Sistine Chapel
- ❑ preserve my eggs for the future
- ❑ earn a starting spot on the team
- ❑ have no more cavities, ever
- ❑ redecorate my office
- ❑ observe kangaroos in the wild
- ❑ love my job
- ❑ visit the Biltmore Estate in North Carolina during the tulip festival
- ❑ build a table out of old wooden snowshoes

- ❏ teach a cat to fetch
- ❏ try to lower my expectations of others
- ❏ be a hero to someone
- ❏ race in a 10K and win in my age class
- ❏ patent, bottle, and sell my recipe for
  spaghetti sauce
- ❏ see my high school
  football number retired
- ❏ fly a kite
- ❏ be courageous—not fearless—in the face
  of danger or difficulty
- ❏ see all the Oscar-nominated movies back to
  1927
- ❏ own a genuine Persian carpet
- ❏ ....
- ❏ ....
- ❏ ....
- ❏ ....
- ❏ play timpani in a symphony orchestra
- ❏ win a prize in a science fair
- ❏ expect the possible, aim for more
- ❏ walk behind a waterfall

- ❑ look just like someone famous
- ❑ manage my own investment portfolio
- ❑ learn how planes stay up
- ❑ win a black belt in the martial arts
- ❑ reach out to help without waiting for someone to ask
- ❑ observe a stampede of bison
- ❑ stay in the Presidential Suite at a luxury hotel and order all my meals from room service
- ❑ sit next to Woody Allen at a Knicks game
- ❑ sit next to Jack Nicholson at a Lakers game
- ❑ give—and get—credit where it's due
- ❑ ride the cutting edge of technology
- ❑ be my lover's best friend
- ❑ ....
- ❑ ....
- ❑ ....
- ❑ "do" the Hollywood hot spots when price is no object
- ❑ sit in the dugout with my team during a World Series game

❑ order Dom Pérignon with my fries
   and cheeseburger

❑ ....

❑ ....

❑ ....

❑ deliver a sermon in church

❑ ski a double-diamond trail in Jackson Hole

❑ finally learn to drive a standard-shift car

❑ turn feelings of kindness into behavior

❑ hire on as gourmet chef on a handsome
   millionaire's yacht

❑ own every book ever written on my
   favorite subject

❑ win respect for who I am, not for what
   I've done

❑ watch lions feeding on a kill in East Africa

❑ own a fully equipped, state-of-the-art do-it-
   yourself workshop

❑ load a loom and weave my own cloth

❑ catch a thief

❑ sail into the harbor of Rio de Janeiro

❑ ride on a private jet

❑ win a place in the chorus performing
the "Ode to Joy" in Beethoven's
Ninth Symphony
❑ possess the newspaper from the day of my
birth
❑ seek elegance rather than luxury
❑ drive old Route 66 in a classic
T-Bird
❑ master my tennis serve
❑ invent a picnic blanket that repels ants
❑ see through the image to concentrate
on the substance
❑ see my favorite childhood movie again
❑ jump-start a car
❑ ....
❑ ....
❑ ....
❑ not put off till tomorrow what I can do
today
❑ deliver fresh flowers regularly to the local
nursing home
❑ get a mention in Liz Smith's gossip column

☐ be sure I know everyone in my office
☐ read *Good Night, Moon* with a child
☐ learn to use chopsticks properly
☐ ....
☐ see a comet
☐ shoot a skyhook like Kareem Abdul-Jabbar
☐ visit the Orkney Islands
☐ build a stile of steps for crossing the fence
☐ start a wine cellar
☐ play in a marching band
☐ sponsor a child for summer camp
☐ learn to be a cheerleader
☐ find one of the FBI's Most Wanted
☐ hear a great orchestra in a concert at
    Carnegie Hall
☐ save enough for a comfortable retirement
☐ see a Gutenberg Bible
☐ attend a Congressional committee hearing
☐ raise my ecological consciousness
☐ treat myself to a mud bath
☐ be one of the singers in the
    Rosenkavalier trio

❏ collect a complete set of Burma Shave ads
❏ be less harsh with myself and with others
❏ check stock market quotations on the Internet
❏ tour Wales in a horse-drawn caravan
❏ ....
❏ ....
❏ ....
❏ go to the Rose Bowl
❏ reread all the Nero Wolfe mysteries
❏ be invited for a weekend at Camp David
❏ own a photograph by Walker Evans
❏ spend a day in bed writing my memoirs
    and talking on a Princess phone
❏ telephone the celebrity I most admire
❏ be able to recite the six ways a batter can
    get on base without a hit
❏ dress in an authentic costume from the
    Elizabethan Age
❏ deliver flowers for a day so I can see the
    recipients' reactions
❏ own an erotic sculpture from India
❏ be liked for my inner qualities

- ❏ see the room at Appomattox Court House where Robert E. Lee surrendered to Ulysses S. Grant
- ❏ blow glass
- ❏ round the Cape of Good Hope in a clipper ship
- ❏ build and live in a straw-bale house
- ❏ drive along the Oregon coast
- ❏ lick the filling out of a Twinkie
- ❏ learn dressage
- ❏ ....
- ❏ ....
- ❏ ....
- ❏ cuddle with my lover on a midnight sleigh ride
- ❏ find a diamond in the rough
- ❏ enter my dog in a show-and-place
- ❏ ride the Durango and Silverton narrow-gauge railroad
- ❏ refinish castoffs and turn them into treasures
- ❏ ride all the excursion boats at Disneyland

- ❏ decorate my home in contemporary Italian design
- ❏ watch the *Star Wars* trilogy in a single sitting
- ❏ go to a clambake
- ❏ discover the cure for wrinkles
- ❏ greet spring on the Kamchatka Peninsula and walk on springy moss steppes
- ❏ do my own electrical repairs
- ❏ spend a snowy Christmas in Germany
- ❏ win at squash
- ❏ rescue an injured animal
- ❏ play tennis with a new oversized racket
- ❏ have washboard abs
- ❏ forage for food in the wilderness
- ❏ be a guest on *The Rosie O'Donnell Show*
- ❏ make my own cheese
- ❏ eat each course of a seven-course meal at a different restaurant
- ❏ search for the end of the rainbow
- ❏ be known for my great coffee
- ❏ eat a strictly vegetarian diet for a month

- ❏ make a breakthrough scientific discovery
- ❏ reorganize my work area
- ❏ taste the native foods of every region on earth
- ❏ walk through a door marked "Authorized Personnel Only"
- ❏ be a camp counselor
- ❏ persuade a smoker to quit the habit
- ❏ own the New York Yankees
- ❏ learn to twirl and toss a baton
- ❏ solve Rubik's Cube
- ❏ do as my heart prompts me to do
- ❏ volunteer for Head Start
- ❏ ....
- ❏ ....
- ❏ ....
- ❏ ....
- ❏ buy a stock at $1 and watch it grow to $50
- ❏ telecommute
- ❏ celebrate the birth of a child with a gift of a financial nest egg
- ❏ speak gently, act openly

- ❏ do research in the reading room of the British Museum
- ❏ hike the route of the High Sierra camps in Yosemite National Park
- ❏ make a radical career change
- ❏ join a motorcycle club
- ❏ own a small-circulation newspaper
- ❏ see clearly, think rationally, and reason logically
- ❏ ....
- ❏ ....
- ❏ ....
- ❏ volunteer to assist the Red Cross after a disaster
- ❏ memorize Keats' "Ode to a Nightingale"
- ❏ sail with the America's Cup team
- ❏ win a recording contract
- ❏ stop weighing myself because—who cares?!
- ❏ camp out in every state park in my state
- ❏ develop the kinds of cosmetic products I'd like to use

- ❏ write a thank-you letter to someone who influenced me
- ❏ see the Southern Cross
- ❏ at the end of the day, be able to note five things I did for myself . . .
- ❏ . . . and be able to note five things I did for others
- ❏ make coleslaw from scratch
- ❏ take a management training course
- ❏ write a fan letter to my favorite living author
- ❏ visit Epcot Center
- ❏ toss pizza like a pro
- ❏ pray at the Wailing Wall in Jerusalem
- ❏ let the spirit of adventure triumph over the voice of good sense
- ❏ overhear my work being praised
- ❏ ....
- ❏ throw a boomerang
- ❏ buy a pair of Gucci shoes
- ❏ catch the next sighting of Halley's Comet, expected in 2062

- ☐ ....
- ☐ ....
- ☐ ....
- ☐ own one really special piece of jewelry
- ☐ learn how to work a professional movie camera
- ☐ see Wagner's *Ring* cycle at Wagner's theater in Bayreuth, Germany
- ☐ dine at the four-star Tour d'Argent restaurant in Paris
- ☐ scuba dive the kelp forest off Catalina Island
- ☐ go dancing in Miami's Little Havana
- ☐ grab a knapsack and my passport and just go!
- ☐ collect majolica
- ☐ volunteer to deliver hot meals to AIDS patients at home
- ☐ survive unrequited love without hardening my heart
- ☐ learn synchronized swimming
- ☐ plant a vineyard

- ❏ create a budget and stick to it
- ❏ visit Peace City in Hiroshima
- ❏ bake a four-layer cake from scratch
- ❏ act the title role in *Hedda Gabler*
- ❏ vacation on the beaches of the Canary Islands
- ❏ have a power breakfast with a deal-maker
- ❏ ....
- ❏ ....
- ❏ ....
- ❏ hike hut-to-hut in New Hampshire's White Mountains
- ❏ decorate one room of the house with photographs of my travels
- ❏ live on a barge that plies the canals of Holland
- ❏ produce a hit television miniseries
- ❏ learn to sculpt in wood
- ❏ stay at the Oriental Hotel in Bangkok and have tea where Somerset Maugham did
- ❏ become an activist for local bike lanes

- ❏ keep my mind as sharp as possible for as long as I can
- ❏ undertake a new challenge every month
- ❏ run away for a romantic weekend with my spouse
- ❏ design my own Personal Information Manager
- ❏ visit Corsica, where Napoleon was born— and St. Helena, where he died
- ❏ wear hats all year
- ❏ ship out on a freighter bound for exotic ports of call
- ❏ speak kindly to telemarketers
- ❏ run for public office
- ❏ pilot a gondola along the Grand Canal of Venice
- ❏ be the first on my block to have high-definition television
- ❏ lunch at New York's Four Seasons restaurant, among the power brokers of publishing and politics
- ❏ paper a wall with art posters

❑ make a suggestion to the mayor and see it acted on

❑ build a hideaway in the woods behind my house

❑ stage my own Tracy-Hepburn movie festival—all on video, in the privacy of my home

❑ build a tennis court in the backyard

❑ look good in jodhpurs

❑ ....

❑ ....

❑ ....

❑ ....

❑ scratch my name in the wet concrete of a fresh sidewalk

❑ pay my bills by telephone

❑ flip on a trampoline

❑ cook a four-cheese lasagna

❑ plant a grove of crabapple trees for my children to enjoy

❑ throw a pot and fire it in a kiln

❑ find a missing person

❑ get stuck in an elevator with a stranger—
   and start a romantic encounter
❑ learn to water-ski
❑ bet on a very long shot at the racetrack
   and bring home a winner
❑ see the cherry blossoms bloom in
   Washington, D.C.
❑ learn to snowboard
❑ spend a summer in the Land of the
   Midnight Sun
❑ ....
❑ ....
❑ assist the master chef at a gourmet
   restaurant
❑ get away with wearing elegant pajamas to
   a party
❑ own something that once belonged to
   Jacqueline Kennedy Onassis
❑ visit the Desert Museum—a living
   museum—outside Tucson, Arizona
❑ see a different Broadway show
   every night for a week

- ❑ be asked to submit a weekly opinion column for the local newspaper
- ❑ look *down* on the Mount Rushmore sculptures
- ❑ become a forester
- ❑ write with a Mont Blanc pen
- ❑ cruise the South Pacific
- ❑ visit the Hermitage Museum in St. Petersburg, Russia
- ❑ get season tickets to both basketball and ballet
- ❑ become an astronaut
- ❑ set out lobster traps and see them filled
- ❑ attend a Texas barbecue
- ❑ go to the prom with the person I've secretly longed for
- ❑ ....
- ❑ ....
- ❑ cruise the Arctic on an icebreaker
- ❑ become CEO of a corporation and set a policy of profit-sharing with all employees
- ❑ jog with the President

- ❏ bake a batch of Toll House cookies
- ❏ ....
- ❏ ....
- ❏ ....
- ❏ be a commentator on one of the Sunday morning talk shows
- ❏ attend church in an African village
- ❏ meet a monarch
- ❏ study the perfect proportions of the Erechtheum on the Athenian Acropolis
- ❏ keep a photographic journal of a trip to Europe
- ❏ write a how-to book on my subject of expertise
- ❏ travel to Chittagong in Bangladesh
- ❏ coach a team that makes the Final Four
- ❏ call in to a talk show
- ❏ bring lasting peace to the Middle East
- ❏ own a classic Chevy Impala convertible
- ❏ out-talk Howard Stern
- ❏ discover the philosopher's stone and turn metal into gold

- ❑ get to know a true genius
- ❑ winter in a private *hale* in Kona Village, Hawaii
- ❑ compose a song
- ❑ cruise the fjords of Norway
- ❑ run the Boston Marathon
- ❑ buy a genuine kilim rug
- ❑ earn an unexpectedly large bonus
- ❑ overcome my fear of snakes
- ❑ do a perfect high dive
- ❑ be asked for my autograph
- ❑ learn to parasail on an exotic island
- ❑ be able to appreciate the great classical music compositions
- ❑ finish projects ahead of time
- ❑ memorize Lincoln's Second Inaugural Address
- ❑ ....
- ❑ ....
- ❑ attend all the Grand Slam tennis tournaments
- ❑ climb Mount Kilimanjaro

- ❏ travel to Andorra
- ❏ grow fresh rosemary indoors in a pot
    year-round
- ❏ raise some corn
- ❏ raise some Cain
- ❏ raise some eyebrows
- ❏ address a joint session of Congress
- ❏ install a redwood hot tub on the porch and
    use it year-round
- ❏ ....
- ❏ ....
- ❏ ....
- ❏ attend an academic conference
- ❏ live in one of the millionaires' "cottages" in
    Newport, Rhode Island
- ❏ sail with a partner to an uninhabited Pacific
    island—and stay awhile
- ❏ own videos of all the Mary Tyler Moore
    shows
- ❏ change a skinhead's mind
- ❏ in the spring, spend an entire day at an
    outdoor café in Montmartre

- ❑ do the traffic-and-weather report on the radio
- ❑ be a journalist at a summit meeting of world leaders
- ❑ become a photojournalist
- ❑ walk New Zealand's Milford Track
- ❑ drink champagne from a slipper
- ❑ see one of the four original copies of the Magna Carta
- ❑ go bobbing for apples with Tom Cruise
- ❑ learn to play the violin
- ❑ ride the train down the Malay Peninsula
- ❑ collect unusual inkwells
- ❑ go to race-car driving school
- ❑ see a toucan in the wild
- ❑ substitute nonsense for common sense from time to time
- ❑ learn power-walking for fitness
- ❑ ....
- ❑ spend six months at McMurdo, the U.S. research and exploration base in Antarctica

89

❏ bake a pound cake that weighs a pound
❏ live for a short while on a narrow Pacific
    atoll and feel the effects of "island fever"
❏ watch all the movies that paired Errol
    Flynn and Olivia de Havilland
❏ taste beluga caviar
❏ go overland from France to Korea
❏ overcome all the sorrows life may have in
    store for me
❏ vacation at the Broadmoor, the famous
    pink palace in the Rockies
❏ guess the exact number of jelly beans
    in a jar
❏ be the first customer at a garage sale
❏ usher in spring by tasting fresh asparagus
❏ take a Caribbean cruise, eat every meal,
    and not gain an ounce
❏ repair a broken friendship
❏ ....
❏ ....
❏ attend my grandchildren's college
    graduations

❑ learn to scuba dive in Fiji
❑ fly a kite off the White
   Cliffs of Dover
❑ invent the no-crying onion
❑ build a table that becomes a family heirloom
❑ complete a jigsaw puzzle
❑ ....
❑ ....
❑ ....
❑ attend an elderhostel
❑ conduct a symphony concert
❑ take the ferry to Vancouver Island
❑ have my own roomette on an overnight
   train ride
❑ track snow leopards in the Himalayas—and
   sight one
❑ see the Sydney Opera House
❑ shoot sporting clays
❑ take a course in bookbinding
❑ devise a marketing strategy, implement it,
   and see it succeed
❑ get a huge refund from the IRS

- ❑ play billiards wearing black tie or evening dress
- ❑ cross the Takla Makan desert of China
- ❑ do *now* what I keep saying I ought to do "someday"
- ❑ relax in an open-air whirlpool in Santa Fe
- ❑ own a million-dollar racehorse
- ❑ explore Nova Scotia's Cabot Trail
- ❑ ....
- ❑ ....
- ❑ play the organ in a huge cathedral
- ❑ bite off more than I can chew
- ❑ become an anthropologist
- ❑ sit fifth row center on the aisle at a Broadway show
- ❑ give "no sanction" to bigotry of any kind, as George Washington promised
- ❑ visit Mongolia and stay in a yurt
- ❑ invent a truly squirrel-proof bird feeder
- ❑ taste vintage Port in Oporto, Portugal
- ❑ discover a safe method of disposal for nuclear wastes

- ❏ eat an Australian witchetty grub—full of protein
- ❏ ....
- ❏ ....
- ❏ ....
- ❏ sit with the band at the high school football game
- ❏ explore California's Highway 1
- ❏ attend the women's finals at the U.S. Open tennis match
- ❏ lower my cholesterol
- ❏ make a pilgrimage to Independence Hall in Philadelphia, where the nation began
- ❏ travel to the Pyrenees
- ❏ design my own briefcase
- ❏ live in a geodesic dome house
- ❏ trace the Maginot Line on foot
- ❏ see Angel Falls in Venezuela, the highest falls in the world at 3,212 feet
- ❏ collect all the recordings of Edith Piaf
- ❏ check into the Sacher Hotel in Vienna and eat Sacher torte daily

- ❏ study wild parrots in the Mexican rain forest
- ❏ browse through rock-art galleries in Utah
- ❏ go behind the scenes at the Vatican
- ❏ vacation on Martha's Vineyard in the summer
- ❏ live in Chicago within walking distance of both the shore of Lake Michigan and Wrigley Field

- ❏ learn to tune up my bicycle
- ❏ tour the Louisiana bayous
- ❏ master bridge
- ❏ ride in the cockpit of an airplane
- ❏ watch the experts create an animated movie
- ❏ see today's Coventry Cathedral and the ruins of the ancient cathedral beside it
- ❏ feed a manatee
- ❏ sleep outdoors on a New York City rooftop
- ❏ explore the gardens at The American Club in Kohler, Wisconsin
- ❏ put my own stamp on the way I do my job

- ❑ get right back on when a horse throws me
- ❑ get right back up when life throws me
- ❑ put all my photographs in albums, clearly marked
- ❑ climb New Hampshire's Mount Washington in winter
- ❑ visit Thomas Edison's workshop in New Jersey, where the lightbulb, electric railroad, phonograph, and microphone were invented
- ❑ go one-on-one with Michael Jordan
- ❑ participate in a game of donkey baseball
- ❑ win a chili cook-off
- ❑ ....
- ❑ ....
- ❑ ....
- ❑ ....
- ❑ hike section after section of the Appalachian Trail till I've done all 2,050 miles
- ❑ teach myself to play the recorder
- ❑ fool someone on April Fool's Day

❑ visit the site of the Iona monastery in the
    Hebrides, founded in A.D. 564
❑ watch a family of eagles in their nest
❑ ....
❑ ....
❑ ....
❑ ....
❑ ....
❑ bring food to the victims of an international
    disaster
❑ attend an elegant New Year's Eve ball
❑ spend New Year's Eve in a sweatsuit,
    eating pizza and drinking beer with
    friends
❑ own a leather coat
❑ embrace the ordinary
❑ be the sole guest in a luxury hotel for a
    night
❑ be a stage-door Johnny for a Broadway star
❑ gaze out at Yosemite Valley through the
    floor-to-ceiling windows of the landmark
    Ahwanee Hotel

- ❑ meet Jim Carrey
- ❑ play a perfect game of horseshoes—all ringers
- ❑ start a new political party
- ❑ see another galaxy
- ❑ ride the Staten Island Ferry for the classic view of lower Manhattan
- ❑ receive an anonymous valentine from a secret admirer
- ❑ be able to write the Greek alphabet
- ❑ play in a high-stakes poker game
- ❑ dye my hair purple
- ❑ be a storyteller for children at the local library
- ❑ tour the gardens at Ninfa, near Rome
- ❑ have a three-car garage
- ❑ escape from a straitjacket
- ❑ read *The Adventures of Huckleberry Finn* aloud to a ten-year-old
- ❑ make a tiramisu
- ❑ snorkel and reef-walk in the crystal-clear waters of a Bora Bora lagoon

- ❑ spend a night in a palace
- ❑ visit the Basketball Hall of Fame in Springfield, Massachusetts
- ❑ know when to retreat from the world for a while
- ❑ buy myself a toy
- ❑ make certain I do not repeat my parents' mistakes
- ❑ wear a Tilley hat
- ❑ go kayaking on Glacier Bay
- ❑ wear yellow rubber boots and a yellow slicker in the rain
- ❑ volunteer as a tutor in the public schools
- ❑ own a HumVee
- ❑ subscribe to *People* magazine
- ❑ see a working opal mine
- ❑ have a separate guest room
- ❑ roller-skate through the Hall of Mirrors in Versailles
- ❑ dine at Le Français in Wheeling, Illinois, said to be the best French restaurant outside France

❑ put a message in a bottle and float it
   out to sea
❑ snowshoe at night under a full moon
❑ see a Tasmanian devil
❑ learn to forgive both others and myself
❑ have breakfast in bed every day for a week
❑ ....
❑ ....
❑ ....
❑ ....
❑ dig for ancient artifacts in Kobuk Valley,
   north of the Arctic Circle in Alaska
❑ stop nagging my kids at the dinner table
❑ camp out in the Chisos Mountains in
   Big Bend, Texas
❑ operate a forklift
❑ find out if Montana really is "the last best
   place"
❑ walk through the Andean highlands to
   Cuzco on the ancient Inca highway
❑ memorize half a dozen Shakespearean
   sonnets

- ❏ ....
- ❏ ....
- ❏ ask my favorite restaurant for the recipe of their best dish
- ❏ give my favorite restaurant the recipe of my best dish
- ❏ paint landscapes
- ❏ be a real estate tycoon and trump Trump
- ❏ see the fossil reefs in the Guadalupe Mountains of Texas
- ❏ jog around the reservoir in Central Park
- ❏ see Michelangelo's *David*
- ❏ visit Quito, Ecuador, world's highest capital
- ❏ study Greek mythology
- ❏ cure my phobias
- ❏ design an effective sales brochure
- ❏ try spelunking
- ❏ go back and read the classics I had to read in high school and see if, this time, I can see why they're classics
- ❏ recycle all my junk mail
- ❏ play a player piano

- ❑ win a TV game show and take home the grand prize—an all-expenses-paid vacation for two
- ❑ enjoy a Viennese operetta in Vienna
- ❑ meet Tom Brokaw
- ❑ go to a debutante ball
- ❑ eat a whole carton of Rocky Road ice cream at one sitting
- ❑ be the subject of a Richard Avedon portrait
- ❑ spend a cold, windy, romantic winter weekend in Provincetown, at the tip of Cape Cod
- ❑ ....
- ❑ ....
- ❑ go to an opening night at the Metropolitan Opera, dressed to the nines
- ❑ stay in a medieval castle
- ❑ island-hop in Isle Royale National Park
- ❑ attend a performance of just about anything at the Kennedy Center
- ❑ bet on a winner at Hialeah
- ❑ be a great defense lawyer

- ❑ own the original of a *Saturday Evening Post* cover
- ❑ see every movie starring Fred Astaire and Ginger Rogers
- ❑ pause for a kiss under the Arc de Triomphe
- ❑ go on a walkabout in the Australian outback
- ❑ start up a small business and make it work
- ❑ become a National Park ranger
- ❑ dive for giant clams in a Pacific lagoon
- ❑ write a science fiction novel
- ❑ be the honored guest in a ticker tape parade up Broadway
- ❑ order Chateaubriand for two and Perrier Jouet from room service
- ❑ head a movie studio
- ❑ ....
- ❑ ....
- ❑ ....
- ❑ sail on each of the Great Lakes
- ❑ dance the Charleston
- ❑ pilot a tugboat

- ❑ catch bonefish with a dry fly
- ❑ see the temples of Khajuraho in India, with their exquisite, erotic sculptures
- ❑ ....
- ❑ ....
- ❑ ....
- ❑ do 100 push-ups
- ❑ rid the Western world of body piercing
- ❑ see a mountain lion in the wild
- ❑ travel to another planet
- ❑ fillet a fish
- ❑ build a tree-house office
- ❑ ride the monorail over Costa Rica's Cloud Forest
- ❑ see Rodin's statue of *The Thinker*
- ❑ furnish my home with pillows in lieu of chairs and sofas
- ❑ read all the magazines that have piled up
- ❑ devise a treasure hunt for kids
- ❑ travel on $20 a day
- ❑ build an elaborate sand castle
- ❑ learn to play chess

- ❑ spend an entire day in the library—just browsing
- ❑ at the archaeological site of Herculaneum, bring to light something buried since Vesuvius erupted in A.D. 79
- ❑ do everything with my less dominant hand for a day
- ❑ engage in barter
- ❑ restore an old house
- ❑ spend no money on catalog items for six months
- ❑ eat oysters in Oyster Bay
- ❑ see the wild ponies of Chincoteague Island
- ❑ invent a new sport
- ❑ create the bathroom of my dreams
- ❑ gather up my ideas and run with them
- ❑ produce a prime-time television hit
- ❑ watch a real artist at work on a painting
- ❑ ....
- ❑ rock the boat
- ❑ stop rudeness when I see it—or when I do it
- ❑ trade wardrobes with Sharon Stone

- ❑ trade wardrobes with Peter Coyote
- ❑ see the revival of spike heels
- ❑ walk a mail route for a week
- ❑ become an ace Frisbee player
- ❑ become well known in my favorite neighborhood restaurant so I can order "the usual"
- ❑ acquire the courage of children
- ❑ go to the movies solo
- ❑ ....
- ❑ ....
- ❑ ....
- ❑ drink where Hemingway drank
- ❑ revive a ghost town
- ❑ discover the next Hollywood superstar
- ❑ tour the Galapagos and read Darwin on the spot
- ❑ cross the ocean in a schooner
- ❑ watch a jet plane being built
- ❑ trek to Everest base camp in Nepal
- ❑ wear a formal gown with sneakers
- ❑ join a Hindu pilgrimage

- ❑ ....
- ❑ ....
- ❑ ....
- ❑ come up with a family motto
- ❑ see the Anasazi cliff dwellings of Mesa Verde
- ❑ think how lucky I am
- ❑ build a stone fence to surround my property
- ❑ sleep on a waterbed
- ❑ visit the National Women's Hall of Fame in Seneca Falls, New York
- ❑ dry summer flowers for winter bouquets
- ❑ be a perfect "10"
- ❑ work at home
- ❑ pay homage at the USS *Arizona* memorial at Pearl Harbor
- ❑ collect antique books
- ❑ relive my fondest memory
- ❑ jog along a waterfront
- ❑ create natural dyes
- ❑ stand in the torch of the Statue of Liberty

- study the rules of etiquette—then throw out the silly ones
- order lunch by fax
- do something my friends would describe as utterly unlike me
- have a personal trainer
- build a moss house
- master one thing completely and consummately
- spend a day blindfolded
- help clean a polluted beach
- weave a basket
- attend the Soap Opera Awards
- run a 10-minute mile
- teach a water-wary friend to swim
- throw a surprise party that *truly* surprises
- fly the Concorde to Paris just for lunch, then fly back home for dinner
- vacation with my best friend
- grow old gracefully
- visit the oracle at Delphi
- learn to tat

❑ visit FDR's home in Hyde Park, New York
❑ tour the Kremlin
❑ observe the Corn Dance at the Taos
     Pueblo
❑ quit smoking
❑ gain a sense of self-irony
❑ be named a Rhodes Scholar
❑ visit all the Civil War battlefields
❑ ....
❑ ....
❑ renew my wedding vows
❑ learn shorthand
❑ design and sew my own clothes
❑ ride San Francisco's cable cars
❑ write down three things each day that
     made me happy
❑ answer a suicide hotline and talk someone
     out of it
❑ become a hula hoop champion
❑ drive a Ferrari
❑ teach myself to be ambidexterous

- ❏ go behind the scenes of a prime-time television news show
- ❏ be open to new ideas
- ❏ study the *Analects* of Confucius
- ❏ visit my alma mater when it's *not* reunion time
- ❏ plant herbs from seeds in window boxes
- ❏ visit Stonehenge
- ❏ meet life's challenges, then overcome them
- ❏ learn the aviation alphabet from alpha to zulu
- ❏ ....
- ❏ ....
- ❏ participate in a Passover Seder
- ❏ ride the incline railway and aerial tram over Colorado's Royal Gorge
- ❏ be served hot, fresh croissants for breakfast in bed
- ❏ determine the difference between foods cooked bolognese, cacciatore, carbonara, marinara, and pizzaiola by trying them all
- ❏ spend a month in a Biosphere

- ❏ own a home-run ball hit by Babe Ruth
- ❏ gamble in an old mining town
- ❏ edit a fashion magazine
- ❏ sail through the Dardanelles at daybreak en route to Istanbul
- ❏ ....
- ❏ ....
- ❏ ....
- ❏ study at the Culinary Institute of America
- ❏ see the Viking ruins and runes of Greenland
- ❏ rid the world of fad diets
- ❏ get a vanity license plate
- ❏ see the art of Holland
- ❏ design furniture
- ❏ retrace the route of Lewis and Clark
- ❏ ride on *Air Force One*
- ❏ be able to sing the "Star-Spangled Banner"
- ❏ visit every Caribbean island with a "Saint" in its name
- ❏ party on Stinson Beach in Marin County
- ❏ head an oil empire

❏ explore Mount Desert Island and end the
     day with popovers and lemonade on the
     lawn at Jordan Pond House
❏ stop drug abuse
❏ read Plato's *Republic*
❏ stay in a real Swiss chalet—in Switzerland
❏ visit the Waterpocket Fold, a 100-mile
     wrinkle in the crust of the earth
❏ be the only visitor in the Air and Space
     Museum in Washington, D.C.
❏ jump off a (slowly) moving train
❏ see the glaciers of the Cascade Range
❏ get a platinum credit card
❏ learn to play pool from an expert
❏ start a garden from scratch: design it, till
     the soil, plant the seeds, water, weed,
     and harvest
❏ build a scooter and enter a scooter derby
❏ throw an Abbot & Costello film festival
❏ ....
❏ ....
❏ ....

111

- ❏ use my time creatively
- ❏ drive the entire Alaska Highway from Dawson Creek, British Columbia, to Fairbanks, Alaska
- ❏ be one of a group stuffing itself into a phone booth
- ❏ ....
- ❏ ....
- ❏ toast marshmallows and tell ghost stories around a campfire
- ❏ reread C.S. Lewis' *Chronicles of Narnia* and feel the same thrill I felt as a child
- ❏ do *The London Times* acrostic
- ❏ explore the turrets, drawbridges, and dungeons of a castle on the Rhine
- ❏ host a foreign exchange student
- ❏ connect the two stories of my house with a wrought-iron spiral staircase
- ❏ get married in St. Patrick's Cathedral
- ❏ have a suit made to order
- ❏ spend the week before Christmas as a Salvation Army bell ringer

- ❑ win the blue ribbon for my apple pie at the county fair
- ❑ retrace Gandhi's salt march to the sea
- ❑ live in a house that's on the National Register of Historic Places
- ❑ come up to the plate to the sound of jeers, then hit one out of the park
- ❑ volunteer to chair a committee, then never have to do it again
- ❑ tour the train stations of London by underground—from Charing Cross to King's Cross
- ❑ binge on Cajun food in New Orleans
- ❑ play Ping-Pong like Forrest Gump
- ❑ ....
- ❑ ....
- ❑ ....
- ❑ give a gift anonymously
- ❑ dance center-stage at a nightclub
- ❑ jeep ride off-road in central Australia
- ❑ eat an entire Boston cream pie
- ❑ believe there's nothing I cannot accomplish

- ❑ ride a Kentucky thoroughbred over the Kentucky bluegrass
- ❑ salute a four-star general
- ❑ attend the Harvard-Yale game
- ❑ sell the most Girl Scout cookies in my troop
- ❑ visit Buenos Aires
- ❑ invent a new Häagen-Dazs flavor
- ❑ bungee jump off a bridge
- ❑ stay at one of the huge, castle-like hotels built by the Canadian Pacific Railroad
- ❑ ....
- ❑ ....
- ❑ ....
- ❑ ....
- ❑ have a monkey sit on my shoulder
- ❑ collect a Buffalo nickel from each of the years it was minted
- ❑ have healthy children
- ❑ be appointed Secretary of the Interior
- ❑ fill my Easter baskets with Godiva chocolate

- ❑ have a live-in cook
- ❑ get free samples from a softball factory for all the kids in the neighborhood
- ❑ be a thin person
- ❑ go from a spot on *Good Morning, America* to *The Today Show* to *CBS This Morning* to plug my book
- ❑ stand atop the Hoover Dam
- ❑ do lunch and a hotel with my lover
- ❑ go through the fun house and tunnel of love at an amusement park
- ❑ pick enough June cherries to make a crisp, a pie, a cobbler, scones, and a loaf of cherry bread
- ❑ install voice mail
- ❑ wish on a falling star—and see the wish come true
- ❑ ....
- ❑ ....
- ❑ explore the Sierra Nevada mountains for their characteristic glacial polish
- ❑ do a hat trick in a hockey game

- ❏ read Anthony Trollope to enter the everyday lives of ordinary people in 19th-century England
- ❏ ....
- ❏ ....
- ❏ take a battery of aptitude and personality tests to find the career that best suits me
- ❏ watch the sun set over Rome from the Capitoline Hill
- ❏ author a phrase that becomes a catchword on everyone's lips
- ❏ have an original thought
- ❏ dance around a maypole on May Day
- ❏ adopt a pet from the Humane Society
- ❏ own a genie
- ❏ attend a ball dressed in an Armani gown
- ❏ drink mint juleps in the clubhouse at Churchill Downs
- ❏ see koala bears in the wild
- ❏ sleep on satin sheets
- ❏ win the barrel race at the women's rodeo
- ❏ vacation in Palm Springs

- ❏ eat fresh Maryland crab at Obrycki's in Baltimore
- ❏ be a train conductor
- ❏ find my childhood blanket
- ❏ spend a week banqueting in Hong Kong
- ❏ give a child the gift of all he can grab in ten minutes at Toys "R" Us
- ❏ dive for abalone off Monterey, California
- ❏ grow a prize-winning squash
- ❏ ride a Harley-Davidson through New Mexico
- ❏ smoke a fine cigar
- ❏ trek to the source of the Hudson River, Lake Tear of the Clouds in the Adirondack Mountains
- ❏ ....
- ❏ ....
- ❏ get a pager
- ❏ turn my lawn into a field of daisies
- ❏ go to a beer tasting
- ❏ close my eyes, point to someplace on a map, then go there

- ❑ stand atop Alaska's 20,320-feet-tall Mount McKinley, the highest point in the U.S. . . .
- ❑ . . . and descend down into Death Valley, 282 feet below sea level, the lowest point in the U.S.
- ❑ make it to my 50th college reunion
- ❑ help elementary school students write and produce an original play
- ❑ have my hair done at Vidal Sassoon
- ❑ receive a marriage proposal in skywriting
- ❑ become familiar with the workings of my state and local government—and the names of all the officeholders
- ❑ ....
- ❑ ....
- ❑ go on patrol with cops on the beat
- ❑ swing from a chandelier
- ❑ win extravagant praise
- ❑ lunch on the terrace of the Auberge de Soleil in Napa, California
- ❑ have a walk-in closet
- ❑ drive a bus

- ❑ photograph yellow daffodils against white snow in a spring storm
- ❑ stay 40
- ❑ drive a fully loaded, souped-up minivan cross-country
- ❑ invent the self-defrosting driveway
- ❑ do my duty
- ❑ avoid becoming a slave to duty
- ❑ help an adopted friend search for his birth parents
- ❑ deliver newspapers on roller skates
- ❑ go on a retreat
- ❑ do less than my all-out best for a change
- ❑ assist a photographer on a high-fashion shoot
- ❑ help re-roof a building
- ❑ run 100 yards for a touchdown return
- ❑ ....
- ❑ ....
- ❑ ....
- ❑ ....
- ❑ ....

- ❏ reorganize my linen closet
- ❏ make candles
- ❏ give away a tenth of my income to charities and good causes
- ❏ travel through Burgundy, stopping often for fine food and less often for fine wine
- ❏ drive an electric car
- ❏ surprise my lover by filling the house with roses
- ❏ tour the temples and art treasures of Kyoto
- ❏ eat a communal silent meal
- ❏ join the French Foreign Legion
- ❏ practice self-control
- ❏ fast for health
- ❏ visit the Valley of the Kings in Egypt
- ❏ climb to the top of a coconut tree to get to the sweetest fruit
- ❏ ....
- ❏ ....
- ❏ ....
- ❏ understand how color is created and how colors work—or don't work—together

- ❏ float around a lake on an inflatable alligator raft
- ❏ ....
- ❏ ....
- ❏ own a basenji
- ❏ jam with Art Blakey's Jazz Messengers
- ❏ see the pyramids of Teotihuacán
- ❏ visit Walden Pond
- ❏ sink four out of five from the free-throw line
- ❏ paint colorful designs on all the empty surfaces in my house
- ❏ have dinner with the top person in my chosen field—just the two of us
- ❏ see the site of the ancient city of Troy
- ❏ sip hot mulled wine before a roaring fire after ice-skating
- ❏ be known as a faithful letter-writer
- ❏ live comfortably without being rich
- ❏ stay on a houseboat on the Seine in Paris
- ❏ be elected to Phi Beta Kappa
- ❏ drink a toast, then toss the glass against the wall

- ❑ play the Stage Manager in Thornton Wilder's *Our Town*
- ❑ travel first class
- ❑ make up a word that everyone starts using
- ❑ own a Fabergé egg
- ❑ bottle homegrown herbs as gifts for friends
- ❑ go on a hayride with my beloved
- ❑ dive from the walls off Cayman Brac
- ❑ achieve a sense of balance in my life
- ❑ concoct a secret formula for a line of cosmetics
- ❑ stretch my mind and body in new directions
- ❑ be able to go cross-country skiing from my back door
- ❑ read six works of nonfiction a year
- ❑ sit with my lover on the Spanish Steps in Rome on a warm summer day, watching the crowds go up and down
- ❑ ....
- ❑ ....

- ❑ roller-skate through the Pentagon
- ❑ visit the volcanic Valley of Ten Thousand Smokes in Alaska
- ❑ in France, visit a boulangerie, confiserie, and patisserie to determine the difference between them
- ❑ whale watch along the coastline of Redwood National Park
- ❑ dance a pas de deux with Mikhail Baryshnikov
- ❑ ....
- ❑ ....
- ❑ win the Indianapolis 500
- ❑ come upon a first edition of *Moby Dick*
- ❑ learn Latin to improve my knowledge of how English works
- ❑ create a new breakfast cereal
- ❑ fly all my friends to Las Vegas for a big birthday bash
- ❑ drive a yellow MG with the top down
- ❑ see sheets of dollar bills rolling off the press at the U.S. Mint

- ❏ play "Moonlight Serenade" on the piano
- ❏ read *Madame Bovary* in French
- ❏ be part of the parade of life strolling the Ramblás in Barcelona
- ❏ attend a Navajo peyote ritual
- ❏ fly low over all the Great Lakes
- ❏ ....
- ❏ ....
- ❏ ....
- ❏ ....
- ❏ spend Holy Week in Seville, Spain
- ❏ own the horse that wins the Kentucky Derby
- ❏ enter a hog-calling contest
- ❏ read *Ecclesiastes* to be reminded that "all is vanity"
- ❏ sponsor a needy child
- ❏ spend a weekend on Block Island off the Rhode Island coast
- ❏ test-drive a Mercedes
- ❏ join the Peace Corps and teach basic business skills

❑ scuba dive the sunken World War II battleships of the Japanese Navy in Truk lagoon
❑ act with confidence
❑ learn to slam-dunk
❑ spend February camped on the beach on Tortola
❑ fly into the eye of a hurricane
❑ be mistaken for a celebrity
❑ age like wine, growing richer and more complex with the years
❑ fly a military jet
❑ help save the nation's wetlands
❑ explore the Forbidden City in Beijing
❑ meet Ernie, Bert, and Big Bird
❑ stay at a bed-and-breakfast in the English countryside
❑ learn a language well enough to be mistaken for a native
❑ have fresh flowers in my office every day
❑ ....
❑ ....

- ❑ enjoy the nude beach at the Club Med in Guadalupe
- ❑ turn my avocation into my vocation
- ❑ train in Pilates exercise
- ❑ ....
- ❑ ....
- ❑ ....
- ❑ see a cheetah running across the open plains of East Africa
- ❑ wear a custom-made tuxedo
- ❑ bathe in a solid-gold bathtub
- ❑ go on a juice fast
- ❑ play the bagpipes in the St. Patrick's Day parade
- ❑ ride through the Panama Canal
- ❑ own an apartment in the city and a cottage in the country
- ❑ visit the London Zoo, oldest in existence
- ❑ design an advertising campaign for a cause I believe in
- ❑ recite Hamlet's soliloquy from memory
- ❑ travel to the Island of Pines in the Pacific

- ❏ show my joy and keep my discontent
  to myself
- ❏ know the difference between stalagmites
  and stalactites
- ❏ be welcomed with a genuine lei as I get off
  the plane in Hawaii
- ❏ win an egg-and-spoon race
- ❏ go to a town meeting and speak my mind
- ❏ be a trader on the floor of the New York
  Stock Exchange
- ❏ help herd sheep on a "station" in Australia
- ❏ change all my incandescent bulbs to
  fluorescent bulbs to conserve energy
- ❏ go back to school at age 65
- ❏ visit Sant' Agata near Parma, the home of
  composer Giuseppe Verdi
- ❏ ....
- ❏ ....
- ❏ observe the faint patch of the Andromeda
  constellation, the most distant object in
  the universe visible to the naked eye
- ❏ do voice-overs for television commercials

- ❑ attend a session of the U.N. General Assembly
- ❑ ride on a bus that shows movies
- ❑ be inducted into a hall of fame
- ❑ drive I-5 from Bellingham, Washington, to San Diego, California
- ❑ stand on an iceberg
- ❑ become a firewatcher in a national forest
- ❑ win an all-I-can-grab ten-minute spree in a mystery bookstore
- ❑ receive a Happy Birthday message on the scoreboard at a baseball stadium
- ❑ discover and name a chemical element
- ❑ ....
- ❑ ....
- ❑ ....
- ❑ own a cellular phone
- ❑ tour all the Piero della Francesca paintings in Italy
- ❑ cook in a wok on the outdoor grill
- ❑ watch all the "Road" pictures starring Bing Crosby, Bob Hope, and Dorothy Lamour

- ❏ seek homeopathic home remedies for an illness
- ❏ eat to live rather than live to eat
- ❏ make a speech using a TelePrompTer
- ❏ date an Oscar winner
- ❏ create the latest fad—like the Pet Rock or Beanie Baby—and become an overnight millionaire
- ❏ do a walking tour of England's Cotswold towns
- ❏ hit the bull's-eye on a dartboard
- ❏ bring my own picnic of lobster salad and champagne onto an airplane
- ❏ see Old Faithful in action
- ❏ parallel park perfectly in two moves
- ❏ ....
- ❏ ....
- ❏ ....
- ❏ recognize and live with my limitations
- ❏ dine on a restaurant boat in Stockholm
- ❏ learn to let go
- ❏ find a lost pet and return him to his owner

- ❏ collect Norman Rockwell's Boy Scout calendars
- ❏ stay at the Ritz in Madrid and spend my days at the Prado
- ❏ experience a time when men are from Venus and women are from Mars
- ❏ have a theater designer paint a fresco on my ceiling
- ❏ take a cooking course at La Varenne
- ❏ win at Monopoly
- ❏ bargain for a rug in the medina of Marrakesh
- ❏ bicycle Brian Head, Utah
- ❏ witness the mating dance of Japanese cranes
- ❏ be a publicist for a celebrity
- ❏ teach a child to read
- ❏ remember phone numbers without looking them up
- ❏ eat pizza at Frank Pepe's in New Haven, Connecticut
- ❏ listen to shortwave radio

❑ go to a party where the food and drink are
   ice cream and root beer
❑ visit the national parks off-season
❑ ....
❑ ....
❑ ....
❑ ....
❑ fly to another city for an evening of
   glamour and romance
❑ buy all new pots and pans
❑ jog across Lake Mead on the top of the
   Hoover Dam
❑ put my faith in reason
❑ own my own Lear jet
❑ be employed as a thinker at a think tank
❑ jump in a mud puddle
❑ fish for Gulf prawns off Corpus Christi
❑ create a toy that becomes a hit with
   children
❑ have drinks at the Select and the Dome
   cafés with the ghosts of Hemingway
   and Fitzgerald

- ❑ wear custom-made cowboy boots
- ❑ operate a retail store
- ❑ retain the curiosity of a three-year-old
- ❑ do what's hard, but not just because it's hard
- ❑ breed a hybrid flower and have it named after me
- ❑ attend a dinner theater
- ❑ find a message from my spouse in my suitcase when I'm away from home
- ❑ learn to play the accordion
- ❑ canoe the little rivers of New Jersey—lazily
- ❑ prepare a treasure hunt as a birthday gift for a friend
- ❑ cook on an open hearth
- ❑ drive the 3,100 miles of Gulf shoreline between Florida and Mexico
- ❑ ....
- ❑ ....
- ❑ receive a gift of fifty pounds of M&Ms
- ❑ see the free Shakespeare in the Park in New York's Central Park

❑ donate to a friend's favorite charity
❑ take in the show at the planetarium
❑ set traps for Alaska king crab
❑ convene a power breakfast at McDonald's
❑ throw a party with a pianist playing
   requests
❑ have a favorite poem transcribed onto
   parchment by a professional calligrapher
❑ breakfast by candlelight on a cold, dark
   winter morning
❑ "kidnap" my mate for a romantic getaway
❑ ....
❑ ....
❑ ....
❑ ....
❑ take ballroom dancing lessons
❑ walk the length of Hadrian's Wall in
   Britain—72 miles
❑ buy a puppy
❑ come home to find all the chores done
❑ order a Louisville slugger with my name
   incised in it

- ❑ see the ancient Greek temples of Paestum, Italy
- ❑ spend New Year's Eve in Times Square
- ❑ ride a tandem bike with my child
- ❑ hire a personal shopper
- ❑ visit the American Museum of Brewing History and Arts in Kentucky
- ❑ eat my favorite foods blindfolded
- ❑ reach the summit of Mount Katahdin in Maine
- ❑ join an anthropological expedition exploring human origins in East Africa
- ❑ ....
- ❑ ....
- ❑ ....
- ❑ play folk music in a coffeehouse
- ❑ replace all my LPs with CDs
- ❑ dine on 18-karat-gold plates using 18-karat-gold utensils
- ❑ have an artist caricature each member of my family in a group portrait
- ❑ learn archery

- ❏ climb a mountain on the moon
- ❏ abandon my inhibitions
- ❏ ....
- ❏ ....
- ❏ ....
- ❏ enlarge a favorite cartoon to poster size
- ❏ obtain some Cold War issues of *Pravda* in Russian, and keep them as collector's items
- ❏ study ikebana—the art of Japanese flower arranging
- ❏ play hooky from work and go fishing
- ❏ defend myself successfully in a court case
- ❏ visit Quebec City to get a taste of France in North America
- ❏ declare my love in a full-page newspaper ad
- ❏ declare my love in a tiny filler ad on the bottom of the newspaper's front page
- ❏ ride a steam railway
- ❏ win a wishbone pull
- ❏ leave everything behind for a while and stretch my wings

- ❑ run with the bulls in Pamplona
- ❑ dress formally for dinner at home
- ❑ create family rituals that become traditions
- ❑ drive a black Jaguar XK150S convertible with chrome wire wheels
- ❑ learn technical rock climbing
- ❑ read everything my favorite author has ever written
- ❑ travel across Canada by train from Toronto to Vancouver, spending most of the time in the dome car
- ❑ film a video entitled "A Day in the Life of My Family"
- ❑ watch a stunt-flying exhibition
- ❑ get a civil service rating
- ❑ learn to cook Cajun style
- ❑ tour California's wine country
- ❑ view the Perseid meteor shower in August

- ❑ ....
- ❑ ....
- ❑ ....

❑ double my money in a single year
❑ go through a year without catching a
   single cold
❑ be a voice in a Walt Disney cartoon
❑ run a backward mile race on April
   Fool's Day
❑ explore the Wisconsin Dells
❑ dare to play cards with a man called "Doc"
❑ stay at the Mena House in Giza, in the
   shadow of the Great Pyramids
❑ create a customized crossword puzzle for
   my lover, providing clues that only we
   two could know
❑ ....
❑ ....
❑ ....
❑ design my own wedding dress
❑ invent something to patent
❑ think of what I would do if I had only three
   months to live, and do it
❑ exchange houses with a family in another
   country for a year

- ❏ ....
- ❏ ....
- ❏ eat barbecue at Arthur Bryant's in Kansas City
- ❏ buy an airline
- ❏ go one-on-one with André Agassi
- ❏ run an inn in Vermont
- ❏ shop in Hay-on-Wye, the world's largest used book center, on the border of England and Wales
- ❏ find a cure for acne
- ❏ stay at the Lodge and Spa at Cordillera in Vail and become holistically fit
- ❏ lighten my schedule
- ❏ follow the wildebeest migration across South Africa
- ❏ spend a weekend in the Egyptian Suite of the Fantasy Inn at Lake Tahoe
- ❏ cut a record with Van Morrison
- ❏ find a dinosaur bone
- ❏ dive the Weddell Sea off Antarctica wearing a drysuit

- ❏ rappel down a mountain
- ❏ touch an ancient mummy to connect tangibly with the past
- ❏ be a scout leader
- ❏ know all the bones in the body
- ❏ hear Silbo, the whistled language of the Canary Islanders
- ❏ visit the site of the witch trials in Salem
- ❏ ride an ostrich
- ❏ drink Beaujolais Nouveau in the Beaujolais district the second it's ready
- ❏ kick with the Rockettes
- ❏ ....
- ❏ ....
- ❏ ....
- ❏ ....
- ❏ dine at Emeril's in New Orleans
- ❏ be snowed in with my lover during the "blizzard of the century"
- ❏ learn piano by computer
- ❏ be a cheerleader for the Dallas Cowboys
- ❏ operate a hay baler

- ❑ eat in a drive-in root beer stand where the waitresses are on roller skates
- ❑ own a Charles Addams cartoon
- ❑ visit Havana
- ❑ take communion

- ❑ direct a movie
- ❑ hear a real lion roar
- ❑ win an Olympic medal
- ❑ meet a Medal of Honor winner
- ❑ read all the Ellery Queen mysteries
- ❑ sponsor a kids' sports team
- ❑ work on an assembly line
- ❑ explore the Lehman Caves in Nevada
- ❑ ride in a vintage Aston Martin
- ❑ compile my own box of 64 Crayolas
- ❑ do an impersonation of Newt Gingrich
- ❑ win money in Atlantic City and spend it on saltwater taffy
- ❑ ....
- ❑ ....
- ❑ ....
- ❑ go up the down escalator—backwards

❑ have long hair
❑ inscribe a message of love in the icing
   on the cake
❑ run a six-minute mile
❑ warm up in the Boiling River hot springs
   near Yellowstone National Park—in the
   middle of winter
❑ create my own reality out of the facts of
   my life
❑ be Vice President of the United States
❑ travel with the whole Little League team to
   the Hall of Fame at Cooperstown
❑ ....
❑ ....
❑ ....
❑ keep a pig as a pet and name it Wilbur
❑ have the kind of garden party staged in all
   those Merchant-Ivory "white flannel"
   movies
❑ own all the Beatles' recordings
❑ wear a propeller beanie for a day
❑ be a player on a television game show

- ❑ watch a rainbow till it disappears
- ❑ be part of a community that survives a bad flood, then works together to rebuild
- ❑ paint the town red
- ❑ eat a newly laid egg, fetched from the chicken's nest
- ❑ join a jogging club
- ❑ go underground to see the produce at the world's largest mushroom farm in Pennsylvania
- ❑ ....
- ❑ ....
- ❑ volunteer at a hospice
- ❑ walk through a bamboo forest
- ❑ install a sauna in my home
- ❑ skate for miles on a frozen river with the wind at my back
- ❑ drop out
- ❑ spend a night in a prison to see what lack of freedom is like
- ❑ make the *Guinness Book of World Records*
- ❑ swim the English Channel

- ❑ ....
- ❑ ....
- ❑ inherit a vacation home in the Sangre de Cristo Mountains
- ❑ surpass my own expectations
- ❑ see lightning strike—but not too close!
- ❑ own a Pentium processor
- ❑ name a star for my best friend as a birthday gift
- ❑ enjoy travel with my children
- ❑ be an apprentice to an old-fashioned rope-maker
- ❑ take a space walk
- ❑ visit the largest castle in the world, Hradcany in the Czech Republic
- ❑ make a gingerbread house
- ❑ watch all of Woody Allen's films
- ❑ build a six-foot snowman
- ❑ learn to use Usenet on the Web
- ❑ meet someone under the Big Dipper constellation in New York's Grand Central Station

- ❏ ... .
- ❏ ....
- ❏ ....
- ❏ dance to Gene Kelly's "Singin' in the Rain"
- ❏ adapt someone else's novel for the movies
- ❏ travel with the Ringling Brothers and Barnum & Bailey Circus
- ❏ learn wine-making in the Vouvray district of France
- ❏ smell a salad bowl that has just been handmade from olive wood
- ❏ volunteer in my child's school
- ❏ eat reindeer steak in Greenland
- ❏ teach my cat to brush its teeth
- ❏ close a flamenco bar in Granada, Spain
- ❏ live in a society in which no child was ever abused or molested
- ❏ buy a classic Chanel suit
- ❏ warm up with the Chicago Bulls
- ❏ plant a single seed and watch it germinate and grow
- ❏ eat a life-size chocolate bunny

- ❏ participate in a bed race in the role of sleeper
- ❏ toss a grape and catch it in my mouth
- ❏ learn to shuck oysters
- ❏ live in a communal setting in contact with people of all ages
- ❏ weave a flower necklace
- ❏ join a Polar dogsled expedition
- ❏ make a piñata for my child's birthday party
- ❏ win a Scrabble championship
- ❏ knit a wool winter cap
- ❏ sit in on a recording session with Rosemary Clooney
- ❏ pedal-boat around a small Pacific island
- ❏ be an overachiever
- ❏ see Niagara Falls from both sides of the border
- ❏ ....
- ❏ ....
- ❏ go to the top of the World Trade Center on a clear day
- ❏ drive a Gold Cup hydroplane

- ❏ pay off my mortgage
- ❏ untangle an impossible knot
- ❏ meet a pen pal I've been writing to for twenty years
- ❏ watch Native Americans construct a totem pole in the Yukon Territory
- ❏ ....
- ❏ ....
- ❏ ....
- ❏ build a house of cards
- ❏ install central air-conditioning in my home
- ❏ learn how to upholster furniture
- ❏ attend a performance under the stars at the Santa Fe Opera
- ❏ see the 114-foot indoor waterfall in Detroit's International Center
- ❏ be a passenger in a plane that takes off from and lands on an aircraft carrier
- ❏ participate in a tractor pull
- ❏ hear buskers in the London Underground
- ❏ paint a mural on the side of a building
- ❏ travel around the world aboard the *QE2*

❑ build an elaborate construction out of
     Popsicle sticks
❑ swim off the Tahitian islands, where there
     is virtually no tide
❑ nap in a tree
❑ own a celebrity autograph
❑ spend a week visiting all 16 Smithsonian
     museums
❑ become a syndicated columnist
❑ twirl a baton well enough to lead the
     homecoming parade
❑ assume a pseudonym that makes me
     sound foreign-born and of the
     opposite sex
❑ ....
❑ ....
❑ ....
❑ visit the Cahokia Mounds near East St.
     Louis, the largest prehistoric earthworks
     site in the United States
❑ participate in a Chinese New Year
     celebration in San Francisco

❏ watch an aerial performance
❏ ride up in a cherrypicker
❏ ....
❏ ....
❏ ....
❏ ....
❏ buy an island
❏ kiss the Blarney Stone
❏ go back in time and have lunch with
    Leonardo da Vinci
❏ telephone old lovers and find out if they are
    anywhere near as exciting as I once
    thought they were
❏ raise ostriches
❏ see a herd of bison on the American plains
❏ keep a cow
❏ hostel through Spain's Picos de Europa
❏ see the Rosetta stone in the British
    Museum
❏ challenge accepted assumptions before
    reaching a conclusion
❏ live in a penthouse with a private elevator

- ❏ cruise the Riau Archipelago off the Malay Peninsula
- ❏ learn to make baklava
- ❏ sit on a beach in California with an orange grove behind me and snowcapped mountains in the distance
- ❏ ascend the Porcelain Tower of Nanking
- ❏ be an emergency room doctor
- ❏ have a published writer ask me to collaborate on a book
- ❏ eat sushi in Tokyo
- ❏ on my birthday, eat ice cream for breakfast, lunch, and dinner
- ❏ ....
- ❏ ....
- ❏ find the quiet center within myself
- ❏ play bass with Eric Clapton
- ❏ get shoes custom-made to fit my feet, which are two different sizes
- ❏ write a poem as a wedding gift
- ❏ vacation in the Cape Verde Islands in the dead of winter

- ❑ explore a junkyard for thrown-away treasures
- ❑ cuddle a koala
- ❑ cook over the fire in a hanging pot
- ❑ be the caller at a square dance
- ❑ stand on the Rock of Gibraltar
- ❑ record my dreams
- ❑ taste *gaufres*—hot Belgian waffles—in Belgium
- ❑ ask questions with the innocence of a child
- ❑ visit Liechtenstein, the only nation entirely in the Alps
- ❑ be named employee of the month
- ❑ use metaphors in my speaking and writing
- ❑ study Shakespeare with the Royal Shakespeare Company in London
- ❑ develop a thick skin
- ❑ ....
- ❑ ....
- ❑ eat Edam cheese in Edam, Holland
- ❑ compete with my colleagues instead of contesting with them

- [ ] drive the Alcan Highway
- [ ] break the rules
- [ ] ....
- [ ] ....
- [ ] ....
- [ ] design packaging
- [ ] focus on the positive
- [ ] ski in Hawaii
- [ ] fish the streams of Montana's Gallatin Valley in summer
- [ ] enter unknown territory at my own risk
- [ ] tour Alaska with a bush pilot
- [ ] design my kitchen so everything I really need is within reach
- [ ] learn to make pizza
- [ ] be a backup dancer with Tina Turner
- [ ] expect abundance
- [ ] go back in time and meet Coco Chanel
- [ ] eat beignets at the Café du Monde in New Orleans
- [ ] ask someone out even though I'm sure he'd say no

❑ canoe the Yukon
❑ find new plants
    sprouting in a recent lava flow
❑ fight my way past obstacles
❑ watch somebody else bungee jump off
    a bridge
❑ understudy the star of a Broadway
    musical
❑ hear wolves in the wild
❑ join a dating service in cyberspace
❑ be considered hip
❑ bake two dozen chocolate chip cookies and
    drop them off at the firehouse
❑ attend mass at Notre Dame
❑ learn cartography
❑ ....
❑ ....
❑ ....
❑ ....
❑ retrace the route of the Native Americans'
    Trail of Tears
❑ own a painting by Magritte

- ❏ ....
- ❏ ....
- ❏ pole-vault
- ❏ pet a giant tortoise
- ❏ get married skydiving
- ❏ learn the metric system
- ❏ coach a Little League team
- ❏ write and produce a remake of *Easy Rider*—this time starring women
- ❏ do my own desktop publishing
- ❏ attend the Newport Folk Festival
- ❏ eat a Kobe steak in Kobe
- ❏ be on the MTV's *Road Rule's*
- ❏ wear violet-colored contact lenses
- ❏ win a game of strip poker
- ❏ achieve a seven-figure income
- ❏ split rails
- ❏ scrape away the dogma to clear my thinking
- ❏ look for the green flash in the Pacific sunset from Big Sur
- ❏ meet my deadlines

- ❑ spend Christmas in England
- ❑ keep my own teeth till I die
- ❑ see the full moon over the Great Salt Lake
- ❑ really get to know every painting in my favorite museum—even if it takes a lifetime of visits
- ❑ own a secret decoder ring
- ❑ ....
- ❑ ....
- ❑ ....
- ❑ write my memoirs in a Parisian garret room
- ❑ beat the competition in my profession and my personal life
- ❑ visit Piazza Armerina in Sicily to see the Roman mosaics of "bikini"-clad women
- ❑ learn the language of my ancestors
- ❑ become a high-school drama teacher and have the students stage a full season of plays
- ❑ accept my physical limitations
- ❑ create a name, logo, and label and sell my home-brewed beer locally

- ❏ be known for one sensational recipe
- ❏ throw a 50th wedding anniversary party for my parents
- ❏ live to celebrate my own 50th wedding anniversary
- ❏ reside in a town with a population of less than one thousand
- ❏ act with a local repertory theater
- ❏ spend a winter as a ski bum in Utah
- ❏ build a large, tiled bathroom including Jacuzzi, double-head shower, and room for a treadmill
- ❏ work for a cutting-edge company
- ❏ spend a week cooking with Marcella Hazan in Tuscany
- ❏ endow a wing at the American Museum of Folk Art
- ❏ ....
- ❏ ....
- ❏ ....
- ❏ visit the Haskell Opera House—half in Vermont and half in Canada

- ❑ act on my hunches
- ❑ live in a castle with a moat
- ❑ build a backyard gazebo as a setting for my children's weddings
- ❑ take a barge down the St. Croix National Scenic Riverway
- ❑ own a Saab convertible
- ❑ campaign to outlaw handguns
- ❑ ice-fish and go snowmobiling in Lapland
- ❑ birdie nine of 18 holes
- ❑ on a late summer's night, lie with my love in a high mountain meadow and count the shooting stars
- ❑ cruise the islands of Indonesia in a junk
- ❑ play a 10,000-pipe organ
- ❑ get through to a Tech Support number on the first ring
- ❑ lift weights
- ❑ live in a climate where I can dry laundry on the line all year round
- ❑ ....
- ❑ ....

- ❑ learn tae kwon do
- ❑ see the Parthenon frieze in the British Museum
- ❑ debate Margaret Thatcher
- ❑ convert the garage into a private study
- ❑ discover all my family's secrets
- ❑ visit the Alhambra on a hot day and cool off by its magnificent fountain
- ❑ run an antiquarian bookshop
- ❑ ....
- ❑ ....
- ❑ ....
- ❑ ....
- ❑ see one of my children attend my alma mater—and get better grades than I did
- ❑ drive a snowplow
- ❑ have dinner with Kofi Annan
- ❑ jog around Tiananmen Square
- ❑ take an aromatherapy bath
- ❑ visit the ice fields of Jasper National Park on the border of British Columbia and Alberta

- ❏ cuddle a baby chimpanzee
- ❏ search for rare plant species in the Amazon rain forest
- ❏ see a springbok leap
- ❏ ....
- ❏ ....
- ❏ ....
- ❏ ....
- ❏ ....
- ❏ ....
- ❏ spend a summer going from music festival to music festival
- ❏ experience my love growing old with me, believing that "the best is yet to be"
- ❏ eat caviar and blini at Gum's Department Store in Moscow
- ❏ become a performance artist
- ❏ wear a Panama hat and a white linen suit
- ❏ ride the gondola to the top of Mount Killington, then walk down
- ❏ celebrate the holidays of all the religions
- ❏ learn to swandive

- ❑ balance the U.S. budget
- ❑ demonstrate the ability to articulate problems—then solve them
- ❑ dine aboard the *Queen Mary* berthed at Long Beach, California
- ❑ celebrate joy
- ❑ buy a really expensive bottle of champagne to drink on New Year's Eve
- ❑ be a teacher for a day
- ❑ explore the Mount Hood Scenic Loop from Portland to the Columbia Gorge
- ❑ play the stock market
- ❑ see our nation's capital from the top of the Washington Monument
- ❑ contribute an article to a popular magazine
- ❑ have a medieval feast in a replica of a European castle in Kissimmee, Florida
- ❑ continue my education—for the rest of my life
- ❑ watch my grandparents board their boat for America
- ❑ fly in an open-cockpit airplane

- ❏ attend a session of the U.S. Senate
- ❏ ....
- ❏ ....
- ❏ take up strength training
- ❏ eat she-crab soup and benne wafers in Charleston, South Carolina
- ❏ learn reflexology
- ❏ go onstage on amateur night at the local comedy club
- ❏ stroll among wildflowers in the Blue Ridge Mountains
- ❏ spend a summer Sunday browsing for antiques in the Connecticut countryside
- ❏ eat the worm in the tequila bottle
- ❏ keep a notebook handy to catch my thoughts before they get away
- ❏ spend a secret weekend with Jean-Paul Belmondo
- ❏ explore the Anasazi ruins in Chaco Canyon
- ❏ restore a classic car
- ❏ edit a small-town newspaper
- ❏ own a vintage "woody" station wagon

- ❑ explore the Everglades by airboat
- ❑ be a beekeeper
- ❑ plant a tree for each of my children

- ❑ listen to my inner voice and follow it
- ❑ spend the weekend at a country inn in the Berkshires
- ❑ look for dolphins at Cape Hatteras National Seashore
- ❑ be a guest on Letterman or Leno
- ❑ own a vineyard in sight of the sea
- ❑ learn how to do painted finishes on furniture
- ❑ take a dinner cruise out of Palm Beach
- ❑ try to make a dream a reality
- ❑ skate in the Ice Capades
- ❑ watch the world go by from a sidewalk café
- ❑ ....
- ❑ ....
- ❑ ....
- ❑ ....

❑ ....
❑ ....
❑ own a '57 Chevrolet with a two-tone
   turquoise finish
❑ be the first female ice-skater to land a
   quadruple jump
❑ eat a thousand-year-old egg
❑ make friends with an elderly neighbor
❑ get up early enough to join "the regulars" for
   breakfast at the local coffee shop
❑ become a harbor pilot
❑ pick wildflowers on Mount
   Rainier
❑ climb Masada on the shore of
   the Dead Sea
❑ drink a bottle of wine that's older than I am
❑ spend a winter week in a backwoods chalet
   complete with fireplace and hot tub
❑ wear a gardenia in my hair
❑ learn how to influence the content of my
   dreams
❑ encourage a kid to stay in school

- ❑ visit Fatehpur Sikri in India, a masterpiece of Moghul architecture
- ❑ be in the stands for a no-hitter
- ❑ sponsor the high school's senior class trip
- ❑ go on an archaeological dig in Guatemala
- ❑ ride a horse on a deserted beach in Baja California
- ❑ visit the Hermitage, home of Andrew Jackson
- ❑ be invited to join Mensa
- ❑ attend the Cottonwoods Festival in Casper, Wyoming
- ❑ stop snoring
- ❑ tour America's military academies
- ❑ walk the Enchanted Trail near Chattanooga
- ❑ collect the stamps of foreign nations
- ❑ stroll through the old section of Stockholm at night

- ❑ ....
- ❑ ....
- ❑ ....

- ❑ ....
- ❑ ....
- ❑ ....
- ❑ ....
- ❑ ....
- ❑ browse through Moe's Bookstore in Berkeley
- ❑ take a helicopter tour over the Great Smoky Mountains
- ❑ hone my decision-making skills
- ❑ live to see the end of poverty
- ❑ windsurf the Columbia River
- ❑ learn enough geology to know if a rock is sedimentary, metamorphic, or igneous
- ❑ cruise the old-fashioned taverns of Juneau, Alaska
- ❑ witness a change of century
- ❑ photograph the sky at Albuquerque's balloon festival
- ❑ pet a llama
- ❑ visit a chocolate factory and collect free samples

- ❏ scuba dive in the Channel Islands National Park
- ❏ design personal information management software that becomes the standard
- ❏ be chosen to sing the national anthem at the ballpark
- ❏ attend my 20th high-school reunion looking better than I did 20 years ago
- ❏ learn ventriloquism
- ❏ be a television weatherperson
- ❏ earn recognition and respect for what I do
- ❏ sail Lake Annecy in France
- ❏ be able to write clever occasional poetry for family events
- ❏ dance with Savion Glover
- ❏ breed sheepdogs
- ❏ listen to jazz and blues in Memphis
- ❏ pick coffee beans in Brazil
- ❏ spend a season as a crew member on a cruise ship
- ❏ enter a demolition derby

- ❏ take my company public
- ❏ live to see the discovery of other life forms in the universe
- ❏ become a volunteer firefighter
- ❏ know the names and dates of all the U.S. presidents—in order
- ❏ make my own furniture in my own woodworking shop
- ❏ smell the lavender in fields of Provence
- ❏ build a miniature Christmas village out of papier-mâché
- ❏ dare to ask outrageous questions
- ❏ refurbish old houses, then sell them
- ❏ retrace the Pacific voyages of Captain Cook in my own sailboat
- ❏ play beach volleyball
- ❏ walk the Yorkshire moors
- ❏ move back to the place where I grew up
- ❏ volunteer at the local nursing home
- ❏ ....
- ❏ ....
- ❏ ....

- ❑ find the highest and lowest points in my own state
- ❑ be surprised by my children
- ❑ hear a concert at the Roman amphitheater in Verona, Italy
- ❑ go to a tailor in Hong Kong and have my favorite article of clothing copied in different fabrics
- ❑ buy a painting from a starving artist
- ❑ teach a child to ride a two-wheeler
- ❑ ....
- ❑ ....
- ❑ visit Barcelona and sit on one of Antonio Gaudí's mosaic benches
- ❑ smell Florida's night-blooming jasmine
- ❑ be an extra in a Hollywood blockbuster
- ❑ pilot a hot-air balloon across the English Channel
- ❑ build a post-and-beam structure
- ❑ be appointed ambassador to Monaco
- ❑ volunteer at a National Park, freeing a ranger for backcountry duty

- ❑ spin a globe, put my finger on a spot, and go
- ❑ swim in the lagoons of the Maldives
- ❑ buy a brand-new house
- ❑ embrace change in society and in my life
- ❑ learn CPR—and use it to save a life
- ❑ invent a new food combination
- ❑ pan for gold in Sutter's Creek
- ❑ own a collection of exotic butterflies from the South American jungle
- ❑ fit into my old military uniform to march in the Memorial Day parade
- ❑ become a city-desk editor
- ❑ tour the Alamo
- ❑ direct a performance of the local theater company
- ❑ ....
- ❑ ....
- ❑ scull on the Schuylkill River near Philadelphia
- ❑ succeed in being content at work and at home

❑ snorkel in Cozumel
❑ start a tradition of celebrating half-birthdays
❑ show my dog at the prestigious American
    Kennel Club dog show at Madison
    Square Garden
❑ live in a beach house with sand for a
    front yard
❑ ....
❑ ....
❑ ....
❑ eat at Chez Panisse in California
❑ stay in bed all day on a Sunday
❑ invent a way to generate cheap, non-
    polluting energy on a large scale
❑ purchase a cemetery plot
❑ visit the FDR Memorial in Washington
❑ convince land developers that wetlands and
    deserts are not simply empty space
❑ coin a phrase
❑ climb Diamond Head in Hawaii
❑ attend a vintage car rally
❑ take underwater photographs

- ❏ join the local Polar Bear Club and swim on New Year's Day
- ❏ own one of the brilliantly colored paintings made by Haitian artists
- ❏ become a college president
- ❏ bike the route of this year's Tour de France
- ❏ be a role model for a younger person
- ❏ marry on February 29, in a Leap Year
- ❏ see the mysterious Marfa Lights in West Texas
- ❏ build a log cabin playhouse for my children
- ❏ carry the Olympic torch
- ❏ see a retrospective exhibit of Norman Rockwell's art

- ❏ tour the gardens of South Carolina's historic Magnolia Plantation
- ❏ make bail
- ❏ write the lyrics to a passionate love song
- ❏ search for buried treasure off the North Carolina coast
- ❏ attain wisdom

- ❏ put my Christmas card and gift list on computer
- ❏ smoke a corncob pipe
- ❏ carve an ice sculpture at the Dartmouth College Winter Carnival
- ❏ use my life wisely
- ❏ become active in volunteer work so as to pay my debt to the community
- ❏ enjoy après-ski chic in Aspen
- ❏ be a guest at a party in Chicago's John Hancock Center—and look down on the Loop
- ❏ learn a foreign language, using a computer
- ❏ tour the Oregon Caves National Monument and touch the stalagmites
- ❏ produce a documentary for public television
- ❏ attend a poetry reading
- ❏ ....
- ❏ ....
- ❏ ....
- ❏ ....

❏ work on a snow sculpture in International
    Falls, Minnesota

❏ ....

❏ ....

❏ ....

❏ ....

❏ perform chamber music

❏ see the ancient Khmer capital of Angkor
    Wat in Cambodia

❏ be the "am" in a pro-am golf tournament

❏ have my handwriting analyzed

❏ celebrate Midwinter's Day on February 6
    with a steak dinner in a cozy inn

❏ sell a screenplay to Steven Spielberg

❏ live in a house where I fall asleep to the
    sound of waves crashing against rocks

❏ play in a broomball tournament

❏ serve on my town's zoning board

❏ fly to Norway for the Northern Lights
    Festival . . .

❏ . . . then celebrate sunshine in the Kalahari
    Desert

- ❏ take a class in neuromuscular integrated activity
- ❏ go to a costume ball dressed as Wonder Woman
- ❏ grow an aloe plant and use it for its healing properties
- ❏ live in a cave
- ❏ tour Puget Sound by boat
- ❏ hear opportunity knocking
- ❏ ride horseback in Tesuque, New Mexico
- ❏ schedule a computer-disk cleaning once a month to get rid of old files and no-longer-used programs
- ❏ ....
- ❏ ....
- ❏ possess an extraordinary talent in one of the creative arts
- ❏ discover a truly effective mosquito repellent
- ❏ own a baseball team
- ❏ experiment with new ideas in how I dress
- ❏ visit the planet of my choice

- ❑ compile a funniest home video of my own family
- ❑ canoe the Coosa River in Georgia to where it joins the Tallapoosa in Alabama
- ❑ run an old-fashioned soda fountain
- ❑ be serenaded in Majorca
- ❑ spend a summer evening drinking Portuguese *vinho verde*—green wine— with a friend
- ❑ become an expert sauce chef
- ❑ produce a music video with Michael Jackson
- ❑ ....
- ❑ ....
- ❑ cross the Sahara on a camel
- ❑ visit Brasília
- ❑ eat Arctic char
- ❑ live without regrets
- ❑ lunch on smorgasbord at Copenhagen's Hotel Royal
- ❑ take time off from my career to raise my children

- ❑ wear socks that don't match and two different earrings
- ❑ ....
- ❑ ....
- ❑ ....
- ❑ be willing to walk out of bad movies
- ❑ accept my financial status
- ❑ be a harbor pilot in Vancouver
- ❑ make a collage of my baby pictures
- ❑ climb Mauna Kea in Hawaii
- ❑ drive in a Grand Prix auto race
- ❑ predict which movie will be next year's blockbuster
- ❑ meet my favorite radio personality
- ❑ instill hope
- ❑ take a carriage ride through elegant St. Augustine, Florida
- ❑ ride double-decker buses all over London
- ❑ publish a good-news-only newspaper
- ❑ teach a parrot to talk
- ❑ see the fountains of the Villa d'Este at Tivoli, outside Rome

❏ work a four-day week
❏ live to play all the sequels to Myst and
    Doom on my home computer
❏ ....
❏ ....
❏ ....
❏ ....
❏ win a pizza-eating contest
❏ rent the Galactic Fantasy suite at the
    Crystal Palace Resort in the Bahamas
❏ keep the keys to the first house I ever
    owned
❏ witness the caribou migration to the Arctic
    National Wildlife Refuge
❏ eat pralines in New Orleans
❏ own a rosary blessed by the Pope
❏ visit Lake Baikal in Russia, deepest
    continental body of water in the world
❏ win an argument with my father
❏ volunteer to take an elderly neighbor to the
    supermarket when I go shopping
❏ live each day according to the Golden Rule

- ❏ keep a log of all the wonders of nature I experience
- ❏ try something new every day
- ❏ paint with watercolors
- ❏ be asked for advice by a respected expert in my field
- ❏ meditate in a Zen garden
- ❏ row a coracle in Wales
- ❏ attend another performance of *La Boheme*—even if I do start crying at the overture
- ❏ ....
- ❏ ....
- ❏ get caught in the rain
- ❏ take a gardening course at my local botanical garden
- ❏ be the only person in the Louisiana Super Dome
- ❏ go the extra mile
- ❏ make muffins from wild Maine blueberries I've picked myself
- ❏ hire a chauffeur

- ❏ see the natural rock chimneys of Cappadocia
- ❏ have a late, candlelit supper for two: caviar, vodka, and chocolate mousse
- ❏ lie in the hammock while someone else spring-cleans my house
- ❏ take a bubble bath in the middle of the day
- ❏ visit the Flume waterfall in New Hampshire
- ❏ send a thank-you note to my child's teacher
- ❏ ski down a mountain in fresh snow
- ❏ drive from Miami to Key West and get there at sunset
- ❏ eat hot dogs and French fries at the original Nathan's in Coney Island
- ❏ sleep on the Acropolis
- ❏ live in a society that has no need for lawyers
- ❏ find a gold mine
- ❏ vacation at the palatial Eden Roc on the French Riviera

❑ ride a vintage Harley-Davidson across
   Canada

❑ ....

❑ ....

❑ ....

❑ ....

❑ be the grandparent of twins

❑ train for a pentathlon

❑ find a marriage proposal folded into my
   morning paper

❑ write my autobiography

❑ see the new independent films at the
   Sundance Film Festival

❑ take part in the 500-mile sled dog
   endurance race along the shore of
   Lake Superior

❑ hunt for antiques at the West London Fair

❑ send fresh Florida fruit to Montana friends
   in January

❑ enjoy the space and silence of privacy in a
   room of my own

❑ enter a quilting bee

- ❑ visit the turtle sanctuary in the outer Seychelles
- ❑ attend the Paris fashion shows
- ❑ have fresh tomatoes in my salad all summer long
- ❑ conquer my fears
- ❑ explore the constellations through the telescope of a great observatory
- ❑ live in a house with a fireplace in every room
- ❑ ride a bucking bronco
- ❑ eschew superstition
- ❑ explore the country inns of New England
- ❑ work as a farmhand in Iowa
- ❑ earn a second Ph.D. to complement my first
- ❑ serve as a juror on a sensational case
- ❑ jog to the top of the Empire State Building
- ❑ deliver the commencement address at a college graduation
- ❑ ....
- ❑ ....

- ❏ swim with a school of fish in Acapulco
- ❏ find my own philosophy of living
- ❏ have coffee in the lobby of the San Francisco Hyatt Regency
- ❏ let the big things take care of themselves and enjoy the little things in life
- ❏ live in a university town
- ❏ snowboard in Wyoming
- ❏ learn to bake bread
- ❏ stand on my head
- ❏ find new ways to charm my mate
- ❏ tour the historic sites of Old San Juan, Puerto Rico
- ❏ ....
- ❏ ....
- ❏ ....
- ❏ ride a horse to a high-country hideaway
- ❏ collect Tiffany glass
- ❏ develop a sound body and cultivate a sound mind
- ❏ visit Thomas Jefferson's home at Monticello

- ❏ have Calvin Klein custom-design my wardrobe
- ❏ be stranded on a desert island with the *Encyclopaedia Britannica*
- ❏ ....
- ❏ ....
- ❏ ....
- ❏ change my first name
- ❏ watch the whales migrate off Gold Beach, Oregon
- ❏ receive an eternity ring from my spouse
- ❏ go back in time and not commit a mistake I made and regret
- ❏ eat grilled sardines in Macao
- ❏ model for a great sculptor
- ❏ make love with a great sculptor
- ❏ witness an event that turns out to be a major historical occurrence
- ❏ meet a lover through a Personals ad
- ❏ get a guarantee that I will have the one thing in life I want most
- ❏ take the ferry across Lake Champlain

- ❑ help educate the public that mental illness *is* illness
- ❑ produce a movie that wins the *Palme d'Or* at the Cannes Film Festival
- ❑ stroll the boardwalk at Point Pleasant on the New Jersey shore
- ❑ hang-glide off a cliff in California
- ❑ create a work that lives on after me
- ❑ discover a vaccine that can prevent the water-borne parasitic diseases that ravage the underprivileged of Africa
- ❑ ....
- ❑ ....
- ❑ eat alligator tidbits in Lafayette, Louisiana
- ❑ see the traditional dancing at the New Year's Festival in San Francisco's Chinatown
- ❑ meet the person I idolized as a child
- ❑ harvest ice in northern Minnesota
- ❑ have a positive effect on people
- ❑ ride the Beast, the roller coaster at Paramount's Kings Island in Cincinnati

- ❏ paint my entire house—inside and out—in vibrant colors
- ❏ eliminate racial prejudice
- ❏ see the ancient bronze statue of the Delphic charioteer in Greece
- ❏ tell everyone I meet the single most valuable thing I've ever learned
- ❏ give each person I love the thing they want most
- ❏ join a singing group
- ❏ spend a year alone in the Alaskan wilderness
- ❏ write my own epitaph
- ❏ invent a liquid face-lift
- ❏ spend a week in Paris, all expenses paid
- ❏ cast the movie of my book
- ❏ commission a favorite artist to paint a mural depicting the most important event in my life
- ❏ be given a gift certificate for all I can buy in half an hour in an outdoor equipment store of my choice

- ❑ have a conversation with Bob Dole
- ❑ help a child overcome shyness
- ❑ donate everything I own to charity
- ❑ ....
- ❑ ....
- ❑ ....
- ❑ ....
- ❑ ....
- ❑ have Placido Domingo sing a song I request
- ❑ find a cure for nicotine addiction
- ❑ travel to Newfoundland
- ❑ become a certified General Radio telephone operator
- ❑ change my worst personality trait
- ❑ take a bareboat charter sailing vacation in the British Virgin Islands
- ❑ design a retirement community for my friends and myself
- ❑ find that I am related to an artist who's bequeathed me her fortune and all her paintings

- ❑ keep my children safe from any and all of the bad things that happened to me
- ❑ eat all I want of my favorite food and not gain an ounce
- ❑ ride the mechanical bronco at Gilley's Club in Houston
- ❑ ....
- ❑ ....
- ❑ ....
- ❑ live somewhere that has no winter
- ❑ retract a lie
- ❑ visit the graves of French painter Paul Gaugin and Belgian singer Jacques Brel in the Marquesas Islands
- ❑ host a dinner party at Windows on the World, New York
- ❑ apply for and get a job as Mel Gibson's personal assistant
- ❑ coach a tennis player to victory at the U.S. Open Tournament
- ❑ reach the South Pole
- ❑ teach my children good work ethics

- ❑ hire architect Cesar Pelli to design my personal study
- ❑ receive an anonymous deposit to my checking account
- ❑ have Bruce Springsteen perform at my 30th birthday party
- ❑ explore uncharted territory in Papua New Guinea
- ❑ take revenge on someone who deserves it
- ❑ reveal my deepest secret to my closest friend
- ❑ ....
- ❑ ....
- ❑ ....
- ❑ spend one vacation a year at the Scottsdale Phoenician
- ❑ solve an unsolved crime
- ❑ be reincarnated as the oldest child in a famous family
- ❑ run into my high school crush and find he really liked me, too
- ❑ hear Sting in concert

❑ have $5,000 to spend at Cartier's—and
    spend every penny

❑ ....
❑ ....
❑ ....

❑ decide what I would do if I won the lottery
❑ unknow the one thing I would rather not
    know
❑ choose the manner of my death
❑ run a publishing house and print only great
    books that become classics
❑ be a foreign correspondent
❑ help topple a corrupt and oppressive
    regime
❑ eat cheese steak in Philadelphia
❑ ask God one important question
❑ make my own olive oil
❑ adopt a child of another race or of
    mixed race
❑ find a treasure in the attic
❑ receive an honorary degree
❑ invent a new and useful home appliance

- ❏ own a professional women's basketball team that makes it to the finals
- ❏ produce a PBS television series on American archaeology
- ❏ design a corporate logo
- ❏ referee a sports match
- ❏ go back in time to observe the signing of the Declaration of Independence
- ❏ ....
- ❏ ....
- ❏ ....
- ❏ discover a friendly ghost in my house
- ❏ find a cure for heart disease
- ❏ discover a comet
- ❏ ensure that my children have at least one great experience that I've had
- ❏ build a secret hideaway for just me and my lover to escape to
- ❏ name a yacht
- ❏ tell a teenager something I wish I had known as a teenager

- ❏ take a poet to lunch
- ❏ visit Ellis Island to touch the spot where my ancestors first landed in this country
- ❏ have a famous neighbor
- ❏ accept the fact that others forgive me my weaknesses
- ❏ tour Chicago's Field Museum of Natural History
- ❏ help reverse a species' endangered classification
- ❏ create a personal time capsule to be found centuries from now
- ❏ find my work meaningful
- ❏ make the sequel to my favorite movie
- ❏ compete in a triathlon
- ❏ crew on a sailboat going west from Cabo San Lucas across the Pacific
- ❏ run a restaurant
- ❏ see the pyramid of Chichén Itzá by moonlight
- ❏ ....
- ❏ ....

❑ write a mystery that spawns a series
❑ be invited to do stand-up comedy with the
    Second City in Chicago
❑ tend a centuries-old grove of olive trees
❑ live to be 100
❑ munch on fresh pecans all the way across
    Georgia, Alabama, and Louisiana
❑ break a major news story
❑ ....
❑ ....
❑ ....
❑ ....
❑ be a highjumper
❑ campaign to overhaul the child welfare
    system
❑ possess psychic powers
❑ see Utah's Rainbow Bridge, the world's
    largest known natural bridge
❑ give my parents a lavish, nothing-but-the-
    best weekend in New York City for
    their anniversary
❑ build a house without walls

- ❏ visit Fort Sumter, where the first shot of the Civil War was fired
- ❏ play Poison Ivy in the next *Batman* movie
- ❏ thank all my best teachers
- ❏ predict an important development of the 21st century—and be right
- ❏ live in a house with an unobstructed view of mountains
- ❏ devise a solution for urban blight
- ❏ drive the Natchez Trace Parkway, paralleling Native American trails between Natchez and Nashville
- ❏ change something in the world that makes life easier for my children
- ❏ pay my parents back
- ❏ ....
- ❏ learn ancient Greek
- ❏ be asked to test the new line of cosmetics from Estée Lauder
- ❏ reserve one night a month to go out with old friends
- ❏ cultivate an ant farm

- ☐ ....
- ☐ ....
- ☐ ....
- ☐ own a Coach handbag
- ☐ warm up with the Utah Jazz at the Delta Center
- ☐ photograph the harvest moon with a telephoto lens
- ☐ choreograph a ballet
- ☐ spend a day riding the roller coaster inside the Mall of America
- ☐ inspire my employees
- ☐ work for the release of a rehabilitated prisoner
- ☐ ban television for a year
- ☐ go parasailing from a beach on a Caribbean island
- ☐ eat prawns at the Central Market in Hong Kong
- ☐ celebrate Christmas in New York and see the trees at both Rockefeller Center and the Metropolitan Museum of Art

- ❑ ....
- ❑ ....
- ❑ ....
- ❑ have dinner with Hillary Rodham Clinton
- ❑ see Juliet's balcony in Verona
- ❑ have enough money to anonymously send some to people who need it
- ❑ launch a ship
- ❑ fly over the Himalayas
- ❑ eat grilled squid in the Greek port of Piraeus
- ❑ teach a child the alphabet
- ❑ be a door-to-door salesman for a week
- ❑ try to facilitate greater understanding between people at work
- ❑ see all the 3-D Imax movies
- ❑ go a whole year with no interest charges on my credit cards
- ❑ collect fresh mussels in Maine, then steam them in white wine and seaweed for a feast on the beach
- ❑ make the sailing team

- ❏ take a nature-writing course in a national park
- ❏ lunch at the Colombe d'Or in St-Paul de Vence on the French Riviera
- ❏ compile a list of all the airports I land in or leave from
- ❏ win a dart tournament in a pub
- ❏ return everything I've borrowed
- ❏ find everything returned to me that others have borrowed
- ❏ train for and enter the Iditarod, the annual dogsled race from Fairbanks to Nome
- ❏ drive a Mustang, top down, from Point Reyes, California to Cape Cod, Massachusetts
- ❏ ....
- ❏ ....
- ❏ ....
- ❏ attend a presidential press conference
- ❏ wear clothing made of paper
- ❏ do the "color commentary" for a radio sports broadcast

❑ see a family member become famous
❑ read all of this year's National
  Book Award winners
❑ tour Italy on a Vespa
❑ be the first person anywhere
  to do something
❑ nap on the beach and wake up tan
❑ retrace Hannibal's route over the Alps from
  France to Italy
❑ take my children to work for a day
❑ identify what makes a vacation great, then
  go do it
❑ develop film in my own darkroom
❑ sit ringside for the Stanley Cup final
❑ offer counsel to those who seek it
❑ ....
❑ ....
❑ design a desk, then build it myself
❑ spend a day in the countryside with a
  sketchbook and pen
❑ harvest peaches and apples from my own
  fruit orchard

❑ consider who I might have been in a
   former life
❑ understand finance
❑ join a book group
❑ list 100 good things that have happened in
   my life
❑ study with a great professor
❑ go back to school and, this time, ace
   physics
❑ ....
❑ ....
❑ ....
❑ ....
❑ ....
❑ study orienteering, then find my way out of
   the wilderness
❑ cross-country ski in Norway
❑ perform in a television commercial
❑ cheer *all* Olympic winners—gold, silver,
   and bronze, American and foreign
❑ go through natural childbirth
❑ find my name unexpectedly on the Internet

- ❏ give a speech to a thousand people and move them to action
- ❏ learn to do the samba
- ❏ open a dog-walking business
- ❏ be able to twirl, dip, and delay a Frisbee
- ❏ swim in Hanauma Bay, Oahu
- ❏ beat the travel writers to a hitherto unheralded destination
- ❏ ....
- ❏ ....
- ❏ collect all the old *Show of Shows* on tape
- ❏ see the San Francisco Ballet perform Stravinsky's "Rite of Spring"
- ❏ like Thoreau, spend a week on the Concord and Merrimack Rivers
- ❏ change gender for a week—just to see what it's like
- ❏ eat lobsters until I tire of lobster
- ❏ cross the Sinai Desert—this time, in a jeep
- ❏ bring *Cagney & Lacey* back to television
- ❏ ride the Cumbres and Toltec Scenic Railroad from Colorado to New Mexico

- ❑ jump rope double-Dutch style
- ❑ keep in mind that life is short and dreams
  cannot be put off indefinitely
- ❑ own a Mark Cross briefcase
- ❑ drive the 101 Highway loop around the
  Olympic Peninsula in Washington
- ❑ see the rainbow-colored remains of the
  Petrified Forest
- ❑ picnic in a snowstorm
- ❑ cruise Waterton Lake in Glacier
  International Peace Park
- ❑ work at my own speed
- ❑ keep goldfish alive for a year
- ❑ visit the site of ancient Carthage in Tunisia
- ❑ spend a day living someone else's life—and
  be glad to return to my own
- ❑ live on a houseboat
- ❑ be moved to speak at a Quaker meeting
- ❑ ....
- ❑ ....
- ❑ ....
- ❑ ....

- ❏ ....
- ❏ ....
- ❏ ....
- ❏ ....
- ❏ own the kind of knives professional chefs own
- ❏ learn Spanish so that in A.D. 2050 I will be able to converse in what could be the U.S.'s second language
- ❏ stay on a junk in Hong Kong harbor
- ❏ store my treasures in a secret closet behind a bookcase wall
- ❏ resign from all committees, boards, and panels
- ❏ rearrange the furniture
- ❏ give my spouse a cut-glass bowl inscribed with the date of our anniversary
- ❏ eat an all-dessert dinner
- ❏ hold more assets than liabilities
- ❏ cycle through Methow Valley, Washington
- ❏ do what I love and earn my living at it
- ❏ study drum rhythms in Africa

- ❑ wrap presents beautifully
- ❑ have tea at the Ritz in London
- ❑ find my true calling
- ❑ be named Parent of the Year by the local newspaper
- ❑ head a government reorganization committee
- ❑ meet and talk with the Dalai Lama
- ❑ refinish my floors
- ❑ train for a triathlon—without intending to compete in one
- ❑ ride a horse through Canyon de Chelly
- ❑ attend a potluck with Julia Child
- ❑ visit what's left of Mount Saint Helens
- ❑ learn to skateboard
- ❑ visit the Black Canyon of the Gunnison, with its ancient base rocks
- ❑ ....
- ❑ ....
- ❑ ....
- ❑ end world hunger
- ❑ soak in an Icelandic hot spring in January

- ❑ help severely disabled children by teaching them to ride horses
- ❑ travel the complex of vaulted chambers at Lewis and Clark Cavern in Montana
- ❑ suppress my inner critics
- ❑ approach a problem by first figuring out what won't work
- ❑ identify a new astronomical phenomenon
- ❑ drink a genuine egg cream in Brooklyn, where the egg cream was invented
- ❑ discover the meaning of my life
- ❑ ride in an Amish horse-drawn buggy
- ❑ work as a decorator of children's rooms
- ❑ shoot off a cannon
- ❑ improve my communications skills
- ❑ skateboard down San Francisco's Lombard Street
- ❑ create a new board game
- ❑ ....
- ❑ ....
- ❑ visit Abilene, wildest cow town on the Chisholm Trail

- ❑ ....
- ❑ ....
- ❑ ....
- ❑ ....
- ❑ coach a swim team
- ❑ see Seminole Indians wrestle alligators in Florida
- ❑ say "The envelope, please" at the Academy Awards ceremony
- ❑ use animal crackers for their original intended purpose—hang them on the Christmas tree
- ❑ have an intimate talk with my mother
- ❑ pet an armadillo
- ❑ get an article accepted by *Atlantic Monthly*
- ❑ sail the seven seas
- ❑ become a Hollywood agent
- ❑ advertise my bright idea on the side of a San Francisco trolley car
- ❑ tour England's Jane Austen country—Bath, Winchester, and "the counties"
- ❑ become an eternal optimist

- ❑ spend a month in a stone house on the beach of a Greek island
- ❑ frolic with seals
- ❑ become an espionage agent
- ❑ usher in a new age of chivalry
- ❑ attend the opening night of a Stephen Sondheim musical
- ❑ remember to thank the cockpit crew at the end of a flight
- ❑ become a radio talk-show host
- ❑ coin a completely new word
- ❑ ride in the Hampton Classic Horse Show
- ❑ see Michael Jordan play in person
- ❑ stand up to my mother—lovingly but firmly
- ❑ leave a romantic voice-mail message
- ❑ ask for a raise and get it
- ❑ own a lifetime supply of Cadbury's Caramellos
- ❑ be known as a gracious host
- ❑ ....
- ❑ wear something sexy under my office attire

❑ learn to make stained glass
❑ own a snowblower
❑ swim with a school of tarpon
❑ travel to the "-stans": Turkmenistan, Kazakhstan, Kyrgyzstan, Tajikistan, Uzbekistan
❑ help transform an ugly duckling into a beautiful swan
❑ ....
❑ ....
❑ ....
❑ ....
❑ stay at the Watergate
❑ attend a graduation ceremony at West Point
❑ learn to play castanets
❑ participate in a paint-gun "war"
❑ leap like a kangaroo
❑ learn to convert Fahrenheit to Celsius without looking it up each time
❑ organize a union at my workplace
❑ eliminate deer ticks and Lyme disease

- ❑ make a pair of leather sandals
- ❑ vacation in the Bay Islands of Honduras
- ❑ cook a perfect Chicken Kiev
- ❑ get an article published in *Wired* magazine
- ❑ build a log cabin
- ❑ employ a valet
- ❑ own videos of all the Marx Brothers movies
- ❑ hike the Tour de Mont Blanc, walking in France and Italy to circle the mountain
- ❑ stay in a high-roller theme suite in Las Vegas
- ❑ grow mushrooms in the cellar
- ❑ run a music school for preschoolers
- ❑ make a map of the town I live in
- ❑ walk the Greenstone Track in New Zealand
- ❑ ....
- ❑ please my favorite teacher
- ❑ go around the world on a freighter
- ❑ travel to Mount Ararat
- ❑ drink cocktails in the Polo Lounge of the Beverly Hills Hotel

- ❏ ....
- ❏ ....
- ❏ ....
- ❏ ....
- ❏ ....
- ❏ visit the Pictograph Caves near Billings, Montana
- ❏ own an Eames chair
- ❏ tour the Rift Valley of Africa on horseback
- ❏ run a catering business
- ❏ make bathtub gin
- ❏ stroll through the Haight-Ashbury with flowers in my hair
- ❏ canoe Loch Ness
- ❏ find my old childhood toys
- ❏ make a bread sculpture
- ❏ climb Devil's Tower, the Wyoming mountain featured in *Close Encounters of the Third Kind*
- ❏ stay in the sole inn on Georgia's Cumberland Island
- ❏ run an independent bookstore

- ❑ learn to build a fire in the snow
- ❑ own a bicycle messenger's bag
- ❑ ....
- ❑ ....
- ❑ ....
- ❑ ....
- ❑ watch the lake of Ngorongoro Crater in Tanzania turn pink with flocks of flamingoes
- ❑ listen to the sound of rain on the roof
- ❑ caddy for Tiger Woods
- ❑ grow corn in the backyard
- ❑ win the Tri-fecta at the racetrack
- ❑ become a surgeon
- ❑ listen to great recordings of Wagner's *Ring* cycle, one after another, nonstop
- ❑ write a play for children
- ❑ experience zero gravity
- ❑ visit Bodie ghost town in California
- ❑ see a Siberian tiger, largest cat on earth, before it becomes extinct
- ❑ bike to work

- ❑ adopt a greyhound retired from racing
- ❑ calculate the possible consequences of an action before I act
- ❑ read this year's Newberry Prize winner to my child
- ❑ lunch on grilled sardines, codfish cakes, and green wine in Portugal
- ❑ float on the Dead Sea, the lowest place on earth
- ❑ be appointed ambassador to China
- ❑ sail a catamaran
- ❑ drive I-95 from Maine to Florida
- ❑ see the site of Custer's Last Stand at the Little Bighorn in Montana
- ❑ make crème brûlée
- ❑ ....
- ❑ ....
- ❑ donate bone marrow
- ❑ attend a service at the Mormon Tabernacle in Salt Lake City
- ❑ take a yoga class on a regular basis
- ❑ create a great résumé

- ❑ live in a cabin with no electricity or indoor plumbing for two weeks
- ❑ touch a moon rock
- ❑ be part of a crew on a sailboat crossing the Atlantic
- ❑ collect old National Geographics
- ❑ walk through Devon and Cornwall in England
- ❑ win at fantasy football
- ❑ take my grandchildren to Disney World
- ❑ keep my photos on computer disk
- ❑ battle a marlin off the Gulf Coast and reel him in
- ❑ ....
- ❑ ....
- ❑ ....
- ❑ ....
- ❑ ....
- ❑ ....
- ❑ witness a miracle
- ❑ discover that I am an identical twin
- ❑ start an art colony

- study a subject in school that can be of no practical use to a future career
- grow up in a foreign country
- learn how to identify animal tracks
- understand photosynthesis
- tour Georgia's Okefenokee Swamp by boat
- sing a Gregorian chant
- be able to recite passages from Chaucer's *Canterbury Tales*

- train a bonsai tree
- sail the Mediterranean
- like Marlon Brando, own a private island in the Pacific
- see Cave Hill at Belfast Castle
- get a seaweed-and-island-flower wrap at the spa in Ihilani
- refuse to compromise
- ride the trans-Siberian railroad from Moscow to Vladivostok
- lose myself in the flower forest on Barbados

❑ cruise the Three Gorges of the Yangtze
   River in China
❑ learn to tune a piano
❑ stay in a bungalow at Ruby Springs Lodge
   in Montana, a landmark fly-fishing
   destination
❑ become a ham radio operator
❑ own an original Parker's Big Red fountain
   pen
❑ taste dandelion tea
❑ eat at Louis' Lunch in New Haven,
   Connecticut, where the hamburger was
   first made
❑ check into the Waldorf Towers and enjoy
   white-glove treatment
❑ have a snowball fight with my spouse
❑ teach English to a foreigner
❑ create my own line of fragrances
❑ ....
❑ ....
❑ ....
❑ ....

❏ reduce the number of "shoulds" in my life
❏ become a book reviewer for *The Whole Earth Catalog*
❏ revive the Automat
❏ ....
❏ eliminate junk mail
❏ do a perfect figure 8 on the ice
❏ memorize the international road signs
❏ play lawn bowls
❏ tap out a message in Morse code
❏ tie a perfect four-in-hand knot with my eyes closed
❏ operate one of the Muppets
❏ get rid of the designated hitter
❏ lose my insecurities
❏ earn financial success through honesty and industry
❏ make real peanut butter in a Cuisinart
❏ broaden my perspective beyond the shores of the United States
❏ cast the deciding vote on a matter of public importance

- ❑ sail over the Mariana Trench near Guam; at nearly 6,000 fathoms it's the deepest point on earth
- ❑ meet a child prodigy
- ❑ fill my garden with perfumed geraniums
- ❑ campaign to save the manatees
- ❑ ....
- ❑ ....
- ❑ ....
- ❑ ....
- ❑ learn an Israeli folk dance
- ❑ buy my favorite cologne in Cologne
- ❑ buy land to save it from development into condos and shopping malls
- ❑ join a tornado chase team in the Midwest
- ❑ invent something with as many uses as Velcro
- ❑ try a love potion
- ❑ shed my own culture and immerse myself totally in another
- ❑ explore Australia's Olga monoliths
- ❑ ignore the faults of others

- ❑ trek the searing salt flats of the Danakil Plain
- ❑ learn the art of field sketching
- ❑ replace court litigation with conflict resolution
- ❑ design a public space
- ❑ join the affirmative action committee at my office
- ❑ tour the fairy-tale castles of Luxembourg
- ❑ check out the Roman ruins and Coptic churches of Cairo
- ❑ spend my retirement as a volunteer for good causes
- ❑ explore the Gobi Desert
- ❑ attend an event where I am a minority
- ❑ learn to water-ski
- ❑ view the spectacular glaciers of Patagonia
- ❑ ....
- ❑ ....
- ❑ ....
- ❑ ....
- ❑ ....

- ❏ travel the Freedom Trail to visit the landmarks of the American Revolution
- ❏ organize a voter registration drive
- ❏ ....
- ❏ ....
- ❏ ....
- ❏ ....
- ❏ ....
- ❏ ....
- ❏ eat fresh lobster at a seaside resort on Deer Island

- ❏ explore a bat cave
- ❏ ask for a miracle—and get it
- ❏ have my cake and eat it too
- ❏ join a country club
- ❏ attend Fashion Week in New York
- ❏ stay in a fishing village in Portugal and eat fresh fish every day
- ❏ shop with coupons so expertly that I can save money for my kids' education
- ❏ dance to zydeco
- ❏ create a recipe for homemade ice cream

- ❏ live with purpose to give meaning to my existence
- ❏ tour the Rock and Roll Hall of Fame in Cleveland
- ❏ be a tester for trampolines and pogo sticks
- ❏ ignore Murphy's Law
- ❏ brew apple cider with the apples from my own trees
- ❏ help elect the first woman President
- ❏ collect antique books
- ❏ speak more eloquently with my actions than with my words
- ❏ cook on a woodstove
- ❏ invent a dishwasher so quiet that you can talk on the phone while it's running
- ❏ have my palm read and be thrilled with what I'm told
- ❏ subscribe to the regional theater
- ❏ like what I see in the mirror
- ❏ can fresh fruit from the summer garden to enjoy on a January night
- ❏ make the team

- ❏ buy a book in San Francisco's City Lights bookstore
- ❏ attend the garlic festival in Gilroy, California—then Saugerties, New York
- ❏ pick a topic and study it in depth
- ❏ try acupuncture
- ❏ ....
- ❏ ....
- ❏ ....
- ❏ ....
- ❏ decipher the meaning of whale song
- ❏ make a great movie about Abelard and Heloise
- ❏ own all of Ella Fitzgerald's recordings
- ❏ read the poetry of Horace in Latin
- ❏ learn to figure-skate
- ❏ find a parking space on the "Thursday" side of the street
- ❏ take a two-mile walk after lunch
- ❏ build a harpsichord from a kit
- ❏ drive through acres of sunflower fields in North Dakota

- ❏ see a performance of the *Threepenny Opera*
- ❏ research an issue using the Freedom of Information Act
- ❏ create lasting peace in the Middle East
- ❏ be quoted in *Bartlett's Familiar Quotations*
- ❏ scuba dive off the Andaman Islands in the Indian Sea
- ❏ finish reading the Sunday papers on Sunday morning
- ❏ bird-watch out my window at breakfast
- ❏ own a voice-programmable VCR
- ❏ ....
- ❏ ....
- ❏ ....
- ❏ tour the ancient Greek ruins in Italy
- ❏ be mayor of a great city
- ❏ explore backroads in New England, as the leaves turn color
- ❏ visit each of Africa's 54 countries
- ❏ keep a record of compliments I receive and refer to it when I'm feeling low

- ❑ ....
- ❑ ....
- ❑ observe the Great Serpent Mound built by prehistoric Native Americans in Ohio
- ❑ study algebra again
- ❑ remember the Latin names of my favorite flowers
- ❑ run away
- ❑ discover the next Sinatra
- ❑ get my news from the Internet
- ❑ have a view from my kitchen of a red barn against a green hillside
- ❑ own an espresso machine
- ❑ attend a genuine Chinese banquet
- ❑ install a skylight over my bed
- ❑ vacation on Michigan's Upper Peninsula
- ❑ own a tractor mower
- ❑ climb the trees I climbed as a child
- ❑ identify my own biases
- ❑ float on the Sepik River in Papua New Guinea
- ❑ take a nap in tall grass

❑ sail the Viking route from
   Iceland to Greenland to
   Newfoundland to Nova Scotia to Maine
❑ be carried across a puddle
❑ try on a suit of armor
❑ dedicate a song to my spouse
   over the radio
❑ discover that they've rolled out
   the red carpet for me
❑ encounter a friendly giant manta ray
❑ wander through the seaport of Marseilles
❑ invade someone's dreams
❑ plant a forest
❑ prepare mashed potatoes without a single
   lump
❑ find a cure for my bad back
❑ shave a peach
❑ pay all my bills on time
❑ ....
❑ ....
❑ ....
❑ ....

- ❏ raft through the Santa Elena Canyon of the Rio Grande
- ❏ visit the Whaling Museum and seaport in Mystic, Connecticut
- ❏ act in a romantic comedy
- ❏ volunteer at a battered women's shelter
- ❏ record my dreams and thoughts on a mini cassette recorder
- ❏ file my taxes early
- ❏ visit the Monterey Aquarium when they feed the fish
- ❏ walk across the Brooklyn Bridge
- ❏ ....
- ❏ ....
- ❏ ....
- ❏ ....
- ❏ teach my children by example
- ❏ participate in my local "race for the cure" for breast cancer
- ❏ experience quicksand—and live to tell of it
- ❏ march to my own drummer
- ❏ be able to name the birds in my yard

❑ see the Hieroglyphic Stairway in the
   ancient city of Copán, Honduras
❑ consult a fortune-teller
❑ ....
❑ ....
❑ master the art of ventriloquism
❑ fire a gun
❑ write my diary in secret code
❑ learn how to fan the flames of my lover's
   desire
❑ arrange a fossil dig for our family vacation
❑ read the fine print on everything
❑ love myself
❑ take a sandhog's tour of New York City
❑ know the difference between poisonous
   and edible mushrooms
❑ qualify for a commercial pilot's license
❑ take a natural history tour of my own state
❑ set foot on the Ho Chi Minh Trail
❑ have a talking alarm clock—with a pleasant
   wake-up message
❑ earthquake-proof my house

- ❏ ....
- ❏ burn candles in the bathroom
- ❏ get soaked in a summer rain shower
- ❏ finish unfinished business
- ❏ watch a bird build its nest
- ❏ listen to a book on tape, instead of becoming enraged in a traffic jam
- ❏ learn to love my gray hair
- ❏ follow the Potomac Heritage National Scenic Trail
- ❏ stop thinking about work during vacations
- ❏ build a house out of recycled materials
- ❏ ring for the servants
- ❏ carve a jack-o'-lantern
- ❏ study how the ancient Romans perfected glassmaking
- ❏ teach someone a lesson about his bad behavior by emulating it
- ❏ see my grandchildren playing with my old toys
- ❏ hold a garage sale
- ❏ take the road less traveled

- ❑ throw a lavish banquet
- ❑ wake up to a rooster's crow
- ❑ live by my own rules
- ❑ eat caviar right out of the jar
- ❑ read the hundred great books of Western literature
- ❑ drink beer for breakfast
- ❑ be knighted by the Queen
- ❑ ....
- ❑ ....
- ❑ ....
- ❑ ....
- ❑ simplify my life
- ❑ see something in a store window on Fifth Avenue and, on impulse, buy it
- ❑ put together a quilt of appliquéd tulips
- ❑ rebel with a cause
- ❑ be greeted at the door with a perfectly chilled martini
- ❑ travel to Egypt
- ❑ grow corn in the backyard
- ❑ do a Dairy Queen tour of the U.S.

- ❑ be invited to Paris by Catherine Deneuve
- ❑ become a Civil War buff
- ❑ join a gentlemen's club
- ❑ redesign the human body for more efficiency
- ❑ slide down the pole in the firehouse
- ❑ forgive myself for my mistakes
- ❑ have a summer bedroom with its own porch
- ❑ watch the sea lions at play from the Cliff House in San Francisco
- ❑ leave flowers on the doorstep of a neighbor
- ❑ own the complete works of Charles Schulz
- ❑ stage my own Fourth of July fireworks extravaganza
- ❑ ....
- ❑ ....
- ❑ change what I can change—and stop worrying about the rest
- ❑ examine a beaver dam
- ❑ explore the Pine Barrens of New Jersey on foot and by canoe

❏ ....
❏ ....
❏ ride on an elephant, in a howdah
❏ organize my basement
❏ reread *Charlotte's Web* once a year
❏ be surprised by a gift of diamonds
❏ catch the view of Manhattan from the
    bluffs of Weehawken, where Aaron Burr
    was slain
❏ hear the dentist say "Everything's fine."
❏ own a personal-assistant robot
❏ call in sick to finish a riveting book
❏ find my lost cat at the back door
❏ learn to shoot craps
❏ build a driftwood beach shack in the
    Florida Keys
❏ not have to clean up my room
❏ take a leisurely boat trip down the Rhine
❏ learn needlepoint
❏ know when I've begun to repeat myself
❏ bathe in an oversize bathtub
❏ study botany

- ❏ be stranded on a desert island with Mick Jagger and the Stones
- ❏ run for Congress—and win!
- ❏ discover a secret of nature
- ❏ be strong enough to lift a car
- ❏ build a winterized hideaway above the garage
- ❏ buy lemonade from kids at a stand
- ❏ make someone smile
- ❏ give a loved one a framed photograph of myself
- ❏ live in a litter-free city
- ❏ ride to the airport in a stretch limo
- ❏ explore America on blue highways
- ❏ ....
- ❏ ....
- ❏ get in touch with my masculine side
- ❏ get in touch with my feminine side
- ❏ own a really good camera
- ❏ install an automatic sprinkler system in my yard

- ❑ wear a silly hat
- ❑ dance the L.A. hustle in L.A.
- ❑ collect hand-carved canoe paddles and hang them on a wall
- ❑ shoot marbles and play jacks with my grandchildren
- ❑ tour Ireland in a horse-drawn caravan
- ❑ take the tour of the Paris sewers
- ❑ ....
- ❑ ....
- ❑ donate a thousand dollars to the local Head Start center
- ❑ ride in a hovercraft
- ❑ explore the Texas hill country
- ❑ beat the opposing team of whiz kids
- ❑ discover that a great event occurred on my birthday
- ❑ sail on a replica of the *Niña, Pinta* or *Santa Maria*
- ❑ remain productive even after I retire
- ❑ install bamboo blinds
- ❑ be waited on hand and foot

- ❑ keep a reserve collection of presents in the closet so I'm never caught short
- ❑ ....
- ❑ ....
- ❑ ....
- ❑ wear a ten-gallon hat
- ❑ see the changing of the guard at Buckingham Palace
- ❑ tour the Winterthur Museum to see Early American furniture
- ❑ be able to wiggle my ears
- ❑ see a whale yawn
- ❑ invent a game that becomes as popular as Monopoly
- ❑ see penguins dive
- ❑ lose, then regain, my sense of smell to see what life is like without it
- ❑ master the yo-yo
- ❑ backpack for ten days in the Sierra Nevada
- ❑ join a synchronized swimming team
- ❑ meet a "gnome of Zurich"—a genuine Swiss banker

- ❑ forget how old I am and remember how young I am
- ❑ see the sacred flying foxes of Tonga (actually, they're bats)
- ❑ travel the U.S., staying in hostels
- ❑ enter a frog in the annual frog-jumping contest in Hartford, Connecticut
- ❑ see a live production of *The King and I*
- ❑ visit Boonville, California, and learn Boontling, the very local language the Boonvillers devised 100 years ago
- ❑ ....
- ❑ ....
- ❑ discover my pedigree and sort out my relations
- ❑ teach in an inner-city school as a member of Teach America
- ❑ make my own soap
- ❑ build a getaway tree house for myself
- ❑ make a daisy chain
- ❑ travel the high-speed Eurostar from Paris to London

- ❑ win a beauty pageant
- ❑ see the changing of the guard at the Tomb of the Unknown Soldier in Washington
- ❑ learn how to whistle on a blade of grass
- ❑ locate water with a dowsing rod
- ❑ affix a good luck hex sign to the side of the house
- ❑ fry batter-dipped corn dogs
- ❑ collect Early American glass
- ❑ dress a scarecrow in the latest fashions
- ❑ participate actively in my PTA
- ❑ whittle a walking stick
- ❑ walk across the George Washington Bridge from New York to New Jersey (or vice versa)
- ❑ solve a rebus puzzle
- ❑ own a food drier
- ❑ attend religious services regularly
- ❑ have the ability to nap anywhere, anytime
- ❑ spend a week in London and go to the theater every night
- ❑ plant a grove of birch trees

- ☐ ....
- ☐ ....
- ☐ ....
- ☐ ....
- ☐ give someone a second chance
- ☐ be given a second chance
- ☐ tour the United Nations when it is in session
- ☐ buy a telescope
- ☐ earn enough frequent-flyer miles for a trip around the world
- ☐ travel the road to Mandalay
- ☐ spend a lost weekend with an old lover
- ☐ change my hairstyle
- ☐ attend a concert of the Berlin Philharmonic in Berlin
- ☐ make a sand painting
- ☐ endow a teaching chair at my alma mater
- ☐ visit the Robert Frost cabin in Middlebury, Vermont
- ☐ follow the government's advice about daily servings from the food pyramid

- ❏ see the World War II battlefields on Guadalcanal
- ❏ understand how the stock market works
- ❏ sharpen a knife on a whetstone
- ❏ share a cigar and a chat with Fidel Castro
- ❏ tour the catacombs of Rome
- ❏ sew a handmade doll
- ❏ send flowers to my dearest friend for no reason whatsoever
- ❏ go to clown school
- ❏ visit rugged Ruby Beach on the Washington coast
- ❏ learn to tango
- ❏ visit St. Pierre and Miquelon, French possessions in North America
- ❏ watch *Sesame Street* with my children
- ❏ turn the family into a jug band
- ❏ stay at Ireland's Ashford Castle
- ❏ ....
- ❏ ....
- ❏ ....
- ❏ ....

- ❏ eat a healthy breakfast
- ❏ see the dinosaurs in New York's American Museum of Natural History
- ❏ transmit a message in binary system code
- ❏ travel to Bali
- ❏ help find homes for stray pets
- ❏ adopt a stray pet
- ❏ meet Magic Johnson and see him smile
- ❏ ....
- ❏ ....
- ❏ travel through the Bermuda Triangle
- ❏ rid the world of addictive drugs
- ❏ fly across the Pacific in a balloon
- ❏ own a pair of leather chaps
- ❏ become mascot to a professional sports team
- ❏ visit Quebec City
- ❏ own a full set of Le Creuset cookware
- ❏ travel by barge down the Loire Canal of France
- ❏ memorize the inscription by Emma Lazarus on the Statue of Liberty

- ❏ ....
- ❏ ....
- ❏ ....
- ❏ ....
- ❏ make a love match between two favorite friends
- ❏ read the 1995 edition of the complete *Diary of Anne Frank*
- ❏ play golf with Greg Norman
- ❏ eat lobster Newburg on Martha's Vineyard and cucumber soup on Nantucket
- ❏ tour a coal mine
- ❏ be nominated for a Tony award
- ❏ rock on the world's longest porch—at the Grand Hotel on Mackinac Island
- ❏ make a landscape painting of my town
- ❏ observe the innards of a computer while it's running
- ❏ see a UFO
- ❏ create my own Web page
- ❏ see the world's deepest marble quarries near Rutland, Vermont

- ❑ make a homemade beanbag
- ❑ become fluent in "short-order" lingo and speak it at the local lunch counter
- ❑ own a golden retriever
- ❑ spend a day alone in the woods, just thinking
- ❑ explore the rugged coast of Acadia in the Canadian Maritime Provinces
- ❑ observe bees pollinating flowers
- ❑ found a school dedicated to the study of languages
- ❑ explore the canyons, arches, and monoliths of Capital Reef National Park in Utah
- ❑ beat the odds
- ❑ adopt the diet and behavior that can help prevent cancer
- ❑ negotiate a treaty
- ❑ write moral fables
- ❑ ....
- ❑ ....
- ❑ visit all the major natural history museums in the United States

- ❑ share a cab with a stranger
- ❑ collect pennies
- ❑ do a platform dive
- ❑ read the *Mahabharata,* the Sanskrit epic that is the longest poem in the world
- ❑ practice tolerance
- ❑ solve a hitherto unsolved mathematical problem
- ❑ visit the Badlands of South Dakota
- ❑ make homemade mustard
- ❑ bring up my children to be independent
- ❑ write a comedy that makes people laugh till they cry
- ❑ learn the art of speech making
- ❑ clean my house with all-natural ingredients—no commercial cleansers
- ❑ study musical composition
- ❑ bathe in the thermal springs of Hot Springs, Arkansas
- ❑ ....
- ❑ ....
- ❑ ....

- ❑ celebrate Common Sense Day—January 29—by doing something nonsensical
- ❑ hear great soloists perform Beethoven's "Kreutzer" Sonata
- ❑ drive a Maserati on Italy's fabled Autostrada
- ❑ hack my way through the jungle with a machete
- ❑ ....
- ❑ ....
- ❑ ....
- ❑ teach kindergarten
- ❑ be reborn as a person with an exceptional artistic gift
- ❑ hold a *Twilight Zone* marathon
- ❑ see a Kodiak bear on Kodiak Island
- ❑ become an emergency medical technician
- ❑ swim for a second or two in Glacier Bay
- ❑ learn to frame paintings
- ❑ visit the Van Gogh Museum in Amsterdam
- ❑ organize a family photograph
- ❑ learn yoga breathing and do it daily

- ❏ think of something likeable about the person I dislike the most
- ❏ exhibit a flair for fund-raising
- ❏ wake up to a whole closetful of new shoes
- ❏ develop extraordinary powers of observation
- ❏ become an Americorps volunteer
- ❏ compile a lifetime bird-watching list
- ❏ defy fate
- ❏ teach a child to play the piano
- ❏ collect past issues of *The New Yorker*
- ❏ paint a portrait of Queen Elizabeth II
- ❏ have Michael Crawford sing "The Music of the Night" personally for me
- ❏ make ink out of nuts and berries
- ❏ gain freedom from troubles and an easy mind
- ❏ run a small convenience store that serves as a neighborhood center
- ❏ ....
- ❏ ....
- ❏ ....

❏ ....

❏ help my mate realize his dream

❏ demonstrate courage in the face of adversity

❏ watch the earth rise while standing on a
   crater on the moon

❏ win a sport-utility vehicle in a contest

❏ have dinner with former governors Ann
   Richards and Mario Cuomo

❏ travel to Mecca in Saudi Arabia

❏ join a health food co-op

❏ be the subject of a love poem

❏ have a conversation with a homeless
   person

❏ become a U.S. Senator

❏ do a self-portrait snow sculpture

❏ fix up an old car

❏ order Chinese take-out
   in Chinese

❏ conquer a fear

❏ explore the Black Hills of South Dakota,
   from Spearfish to Hot Springs

❏ get back in touch with the spiritual

- ❑ ....
- ❑ write a weight-loss cookbook
- ❑ become an engineer and build a great bridge
- ❑ ride the steppes of Central Asia on horseback
- ❑ help make the world safe for children
- ❑ have my own greenhouse
- ❑ walk a tightrope across Niagara Falls
- ❑ read all the books by all the Brontë sisters
- ❑ learn engraving
- ❑ feed my intellectual appetite
- ❑ be known as a colorful character
- ❑ observe with awe the multicolored natural spires, pinnacles, and amphitheaters of Bryce Canyon
- ❑ drive through the inappropriately named Beach, Iowa
- ❑ walk the Roman Forum where Caesar, Cicero, and Augustus walked
- ❑ own one indestructible pair of pantyhose
- ❑ study art in Paris

- ❑ make a perfect velouté
- ❑ attend a Pearl Jam concert
- ❑ learn to restore and refinish furniture
- ❑ celebrate National Sandwich Month by inventing a new sandwich
- ❑ live in Italy for a year
- ❑ win a competition for a public sculpture
- ❑ visit Benares and observe the Hindu cremation rituals
- ❑ tour with a Wild West show
- ❑ translate a work I admire
- ❑ see the ice-skating World Championships
- ❑ live with love
- ❑ maintain beautiful skin
- ❑ ....
- ❑ ....
- ❑ ....
- ❑ ....
- ❑ make a meal of Boston baked beans, Boston brown bread, and Boston cream pie—in Boston
- ❑ own a palm-size video recorder

- ❏ learn a dialect of a foreign language
- ❏ admit my failures
- ❏ eat more fiber
- ❏ win the *Prix de Rome* to study theater design in Italy
- ❏ build a copy of a Chippendale chair
- ❏ ride an air-cushion vehicle across a desert
- ❏ inherit and continue a successful family business
- ❏ paint a storm scene
- ❏ control an empire
- ❏ propose a controversial idea
- ❏ spend a summer in Europe attending as many music festivals as I can get to
- ❏ appear in the crowd in an epic film
- ❏ pull up stakes and move
- ❏ ....
- ❏ ....
- ❏ ....
- ❏ grow a rock garden
- ❏ see the rings of Saturn through a telescope

- ❏ perform in a cabaret
- ❏ be content to satisfy basic needs only
- ❏ ....
- ❏ ....
- ❏ become a lighthouse caretaker
- ❏ attend the World Cup championship finals
- ❏ publish a breakthrough scientific paper
- ❏ dissect a frog
- ❏ rely on my powers of intuition
- ❏ eat a *salade Niçoise* in Nice
- ❏ design and embroider a tapestry
- ❏ become a choreographer
- ❏ watch a dog give birth
- ❏ be familiar with the Norse sagas
- ❏ persuade world leaders to destroy all existing nuclear weapons and build no more
- ❏ compose a movie soundtrack
- ❏ be asked to lecture nationwide on my specialty
- ❏ take part in a cattle drive
- ❏ live in a converted church and dine in what was once the chancel

❑ radiate energy

❑ blow up a photograph of myself into a
   poster

❑ tour the beaches of Normandy, where the
   allies landed on D-Day

❑ start a secret society

❑ look through the telescope of a major
   observatory

❑ work with the most brilliant minds of my
   era

❑ find something to smile about every day

❑ install a home weather station

❑ initiate a program of social reform

❑ hear an elephant trumpet

❑ ....

❑ ....

❑ ....

❑ act in a Tim Robbins film

❑ cross Greenland by snowmobile

❑ study world myths

❑ dive for sponges

❑ become expert in bartending tricks

- ❏ phone or visit my oldest relative regularly
- ❏ have fresh daffodils on the table every week of spring
- ❏ ....
- ❏ ....
- ❏ learn to appreciate Surrealism
- ❏ compose a symphonic work and hear it performed by a great orchestra
- ❏ create fractal art
- ❏ live the life of a Bohemian
- ❏ ride to 15,000 feet below the surface of the ocean in the submersible *Aluminaut*
- ❏ cook on the outdoor grill in midwinter
- ❏ build a stone column
- ❏ solve the mystery of Glenn Miller's death
- ❏ see a grizzly on the tundra of Gates of the Arctic National Park
- ❏ defy tradition
- ❏ take a chance that's a million-to-one shot—and see it pay off
- ❏ cruise the Danube from Prague to Budapest

- ❏ take the funicular up Corcovado, where the statue of *Christ the Redeemer* overlooks Rio de Janeiro
- ❏ look like Clark Gable
- ❏ meet a man who looks like Clark Gable
- ❏ live to see Nostradamus proven wrong
- ❏ decorate my home in Le Corbusier style
- ❏ play semiprofessional football
- ❏ take a nighttime swim in a phosphorescent bay in Puerto Rico and watch light drip off my fingertips
- ❏ own the goose that lays the golden egg
- ❏ be elected to the National Honor Society
- ❏ see hard work beat good luck seven days a week
- ❏ count my freckles
- ❏ find Aladdin's Lamp
- ❏ ....
- ❏ ....
- ❏ ....
- ❏ see the prairie chicken house in Norman, Oklahoma

- ❏ read Plutarch's *Lives*
- ❏ emulate Don Quixote
   by fighting evil and injustice
- ❏ swim through an underwater grotto
- ❏ refuse to count calories or measure portions
- ❏ be considered a technical wizard
- ❏ recapture the sense of wonder
- ❏ ....
- ❏ ....
- ❏ tour the Civil War battlegrounds of the
   Shenandoah Valley
- ❏ master touch typing
- ❏ befriend scholars—for a learning
   experience
- ❏ find Camelot or re-create it
- ❏ have a day set aside in my honor by
   Hallmark
- ❏ say "Open, Sesame!" and have something
   actually open
- ❏ direct a farce
- ❏ serve as co-sirdar—leader and guide—on a
   Himalayan trek

- ❑ dye my hair green for St. Patrick's Day
- ❑ have perfect pitch and a good ear
- ❑ produce a documentary on a subject I'm passionate about
- ❑ ....
- ❑ ....
- ❑ look for beauty in unexpected places
- ❑ make a citizen's arrest
- ❑ eliminate titles—Mister, Miss, Vice President, Director, Doctor, etc.—and use only first names
- ❑ see a hippopotamus cooling off in a stream
- ❑ own a large-button calculator
- ❑ break a bad habit
- ❑ visit Robert Louis Stevenson's home and grave on the island of Western Samoa in the Pacific
- ❑ get carded in a bar when I'm forty years old
- ❑ turn a Buddhist prayer wheel

- ❏ see the Great Sphinx at Al-Jizah (Giza) in Egypt
- ❏ invent a silently flushing toilet
- ❏ become an outdoors photographer
- ❏ indulge my passion for expensive cologne
- ❏ have a week of terrific hair days
- ❏ journey to the ends of the earth
- ❏ attend a championship boxing match in Las Vegas
- ❏ explore the sandhill region of Nebraska
- ❏ set goals that reflect what I believe inside is important
- ❏ ....
- ❏ ....
- ❏ ....
- ❏ ....
- ❏ collaborate on a song with Bob Dylan
- ❏ learn a foreign language well enough to do a crossword puzzle in it
- ❏ hear Itzhak Perlman live
- ❏ sponsor a child overseas
- ❏ sponsor a child here at home

- ❑ play the church organ
- ❑ meet a white rabbit and a Cheshire cat
- ❑ visit Madame Tussaud's wax museum
- ❑ learn the art of animation
- ❑ have a knack for languages
- ❑ ....
- ❑ ....
- ❑ ....
- ❑ ....
- ❑ look through an electron microscope
- ❑ interview Yasir Arafat
- ❑ paint a fresco
- ❑ write at least 250 words—a letter, journal, book—every morning before going to work
- ❑ learn to prepare sushi
- ❑ help keep a culture alive
- ❑ play the Old Course at the Royal and Ancient Golf Club of St. Andrews, Scotland
- ❑ run like Jesse Owens
- ❑ be admired for my sense of humor

- ❏ be able to recite "The Night Before Christmas" from memory
- ❏ live like Robinson Crusoe, letting necessity drive invention
- ❏ swim underwater without coming up for a breath
- ❏ see hail the size of golf balls
- ❏ be good-natured
- ❏ collect vinyl LP records
- ❏ vacation on Cape Cod for a summer
- ❏ be happy with the way I look
- ❏ exchange houses with a Shetland islander
- ❏ ....
- ❏ ....
- ❏ win a Pulitzer Prize
- ❏ greet summer by lunching on the terrace of the boat club in Central Park
- ❏ be an organ donor
- ❏ obtain the autograph of the person I most admire
- ❏ enter the footrace up Pike's Peak
- ❏ learn encaustic painting

- ❏ welcome change with grace and humor
- ❏ tour the homes of the stars in Hollywood
- ❏ ....
- ❏ ....
- ❏ ....
- ❏ go on a learn-to-sail cruise
- ❏ visit the Kennedy gravesite in Arlington National Cemetery and see the eternal flame
- ❏ design a skyscraper
- ❏ become a technical wizard
- ❏ watch a seismograph during an earthquake
- ❏ learn from the *Kama Sutra* and practice what I've learned
- ❏ own a pair of Birkenstocks
- ❏ take boxing lessons
- ❏ hear Dolly Parton sing "Amazing Grace"
- ❏ turn a Scrooge into a generous giver
- ❏ learn clog dancing
- ❏ visit the Vatican museums
- ❏ meet with people in my field in developing countries

- ❑ become one of the idle rich
- ❑ receive rave reviews for a performance
- ❑ see the geysers shooting from Grand Cayman's blowholes
- ❑ own a Land Rover
- ❑ spend time in an ashram
- ❑ dive for black pearls among the Tuamotu Islands of Polynesia
- ❑ operate a dairy farm
- ❑ ride a Sunfish
- ❑ look at the familiar with fresh eyes
- ❑ be crowned prom king
- ❑ sightsee a Jamaican river on a bamboo raft
- ❑ ....
- ❑ ....
- ❑ act like a kid
- ❑ fight ignorance, especially when it is sincere
- ❑ be appointed to the Supreme Court
- ❑ kiss a frog and find a prince
- ❑ drink Pimms on the lawn of an English country house on a warm summer day

- ❑ sail the Saint Lawrence Seaway
- ❑ study mathematics
- ❑ make more opportunities than I find
- ❑ take a survival course
- ❑ join in a march for a great cause
- ❑ get the gift of 20 minutes and all I can buy at Wal-Mart
- ❑ invent a salad dressing
- ❑ make silk flower arrangements
- ❑ ....
- ❑ ....
- ❑ ....
- ❑ ....
- ❑ answer children's letters to Santa Claus and the Easter Bunny
- ❑ learn to repair my sound system
- ❑ marry in secret
- ❑ watch all the W.C. Fields–Mae West movies in one nonstop marathon
- ❑ do something difficult and do it well
- ❑ breed singing canaries
- ❑ bronze my grandchildren's baby shoes

- ❑ in my retirement, become a dog-walker and pet-sitter
- ❑ build a smokehouse and prepare my own ham and bacon
- ❑ have long fingernails
- ❑ be a bicycle messenger in a big city
- ❑ breakfast on sausage biscuits at Mom's in New Orleans
- ❑ stop viewing time as the enemy
- ❑ bestride the Continental Divide
- ❑ attend bartending school
- ❑ live in a mansion in Beverly Hills
- ❑ do rubbings of the grave covers in Westminster Abbey
- ❑ have an outdoor shower
- ❑ fish the streams of the Highlands of Scotland
- ❑ backpack in North Carolina's Pisgah National Forest
- ❑ decorate store windows at Christmas
- ❑ ....
- ❑ ....

- ❏ use the next generation of storage medium—beyond floppy disks and CD-ROMs
- ❏ fly in a plane that causes a sonic boom
- ❏ do the Nestea plunge on a hot day
- ❏ learn patience
- ❏ get 10 percent of the gross on George Lucas's next picture
- ❏ learn how to charm a snake
- ❏ order milk at a bar
- ❏ study hard, whatever the subject
- ❏ be awarded the title Commander of Arts and Letters by the French government
- ❏ experience the kindness of strangers
- ❏ keep a small brood of chickens and have fresh eggs every day
- ❏ visit the Blue Mosque in Istanbul
- ❏ be in the front row of spectators for the Tournament of Roses parade
- ❏ record a number-one single
- ❏ join up with a video dating service
- ❏ ....
- ❏ ....

❏ be the subject of a made-for-TV movie
❏ sit on an Anguillian beach the color and
    consistency of confectioners' sugar
❏ master lithography
❏ see an owl wink
❏ visit the Nut Museum
    in Old Lyme, Connecticut
❏ outgrow my allergies
❏ set five goals for the year on January 1 and
    achieve them by December 31
❏ ....
❏ ....
❏ ....
❏ eat salt-baked crabs in Chinatown
❏ practice what I preach
❏ read the epitaphs on the graves of the
    great
❏ stay healthy and avoid a trip to a hospital
    emergency room
❏ look good in a miniskirt
❏ get stuck in traffic with a glove compartment
    full of tapes I love

- ❏ ....
- ❏ ....
- ❏ ....
- ❏ make friends with people who manage to accomplish a lot
- ❏ keep field guides in the car
- ❏ think globally, act locally
- ❏ have a rent-controlled two-bedroom apartment
- ❏ buy local artifacts whenever I travel
- ❏ learn how to rig a lean-to in the woods
- ❏ repair my own eyeglasses
- ❏ maintain a sound credit rating
- ❏ make a study of Flemish art
- ❏ transplant cuttings
- ❏ see an opera at Glyndebourne, England, where intermissions are for champagne suppers on the lawn
- ❏ spend a day on the job with a nurse
- ❏ churn butter
- ❏ get a cartoon published in *The New Yorker*
- ❏ buy myself a present

❑ go around the world in a private jet

❑ own a red union suit

❑ decorate my fishing hat with flies I've tied
    myself

❑ see the Northern Lights

❑ give my parents nicknames

❑ capture the street scene out my window in
    fast-action photography

❑ make mud pies

❑ subscribe to *Lexus* and *Nexus*

❑ vacation in Palm Springs

❑ tour the Wine Route of Alsace in France

❑ fall in love and burn my little black book

❑ drop my defenses

❑ ....

❑ ....

❑ ....

❑ ....

❑ ....

❑ have a home that my children's friends
    love to visit

❑ attend an Aretha Franklin concert

- ❑ become a teacher in an adult education program
- ❑ think before I speak
- ❑ make weatherproof bricks for a patio
- ❑ swim a trail at the underwater Buck Island National Monument
- ❑ eat thin-crust pizza and Chicago deep dish pizza at the same sitting
- ❑ have the will to find the way
- ❑ weave my own baskets
- ❑ find out that a long-lost relative has died and left me a fortune
- ❑ communicate with animals
- ❑ witness a metamorphosis
- ❑ construct a root cellar for storing vegetables year round
- ❑ ....
- ❑ stencil designs onto one wall of the house
- ❑ watch only educational television
- ❑ keep myself healthy and fit in body, mind, and spirit
- ❑ play tennis once a week

- ❏ get my supermarket to go on-line so I can order groceries via computer
- ❏ look for the silver lining
- ❏ attend a high school that teaches an ethics course
- ❏ ....
- ❏ ....
- ❏ ....
- ❏ create natural dyes from common plants
- ❏ build a stone wishing well in the backyard
- ❏ campaign for universal health care
- ❏ consider cryogenics
- ❏ enjoy a long lucky streak
- ❏ own a chiming grandfather clock
- ❏ be the most popular kid in school
- ❏ explore the Coast Range in Olympic National Park
- ❏ buy low and sell high
- ❏ reverse commute
- ❏ speak at least three languages fluently
- ❏ visit Catalina Island
- ❏ help enforce the litter laws in my town

- ❑ live to see the emergence of electronic "books"
- ❑ write a fan letter to Oliver Sacks
- ❑ throw caution to the wind
- ❑ get a month's concession on the rent of my new apartment
- ❑ drive the Amalfi Coast in a vintage Corvette
- ❑ learn to make tortillas from corn
- ❑ find a cowrie shell
- ❑ go down a dress or pants size
- ❑ do a walking tour of Germany's Black Forest region
- ❑ create my personal letterhead stationery on the computer
- ❑ race a two-person bobsled with my sister
- ❑ tour the private homes and gardens in Savannah, Georgia
- ❑ campaign to save the rain forests
- ❑ have a fine wine named after me
- ❑ visit Eleanor Roosevelt's cottage at Val-Kill
- ❑ live on a houseboat in Sausalito

❑ see ice on the Mississippi River

❑ work the registration table at the annual
 Bay to Breakers race in San Francisco

❑ "retire" my car by driving it in a demoliton
 derby

❑ make my own skin moisturizer

❑ follow in Mother Teresa's footsteps

❑ climb Philosopher's Pass to look down on
 the city of Heidelberg, Germany

❑ found an eco-tourism resort

❑ design children's toys

❑ visit Noah Webster's home in West
 Hartford, Connecticut

❑ define a Rocky Mountain "high" for myself
 by traveling through the Rockies

❑ give more than I'm asked for

❑ ....

❑ ....

❑ ....

❑ ....

❑ see the supposed birthplace of Homer in
 Izmir, Turkey

- ❑ celebrate New Year's Eve 1999 in two time zones
- ❑ observe the Paleolithic art of the Caves of Altamira in Spain
- ❑ place in the top three in my age group at a track meet
- ❑ tunnel through the blue walls of a glacier
- ❑ stroll the Riverwalk in San Antonio, Texas
- ❑ make my living as a professional athlete
- ❑ ....
- ❑ ....
- ❑ go around the world in a submarine
- ❑ master the Internet so that I can claim to be "wired"
- ❑ ride in a Daimler
- ❑ dot the backyard with bird feeders
- ❑ forge my own rules
- ❑ be a guest on *Oprah* as an expert on the day's topic
- ❑ watch the Fourth of July fireworks at the Washington Monument
- ❑ see a ski competition in the Alps

- ❑ sing like Joan Sutherland
- ❑ stand on each of the seven hills of Rome
- ❑ read Richard Feynman's books for access to brilliance
- ❑ visit Borneo and climb Mount Kinabalu
- ❑ seek perfection in everything I do
- ❑ attend the annual horse fair in Rajasthan, India
- ❑ play quarterback
- ❑ save money regularly
- ❑ invest money regularly
- ❑ really drink eight glasses of water a day
- ❑ learn CPR
- ❑ see Hagia Sophia in Istanbul, the supreme masterpiece of Byzantine architecture
- ❑ take a sports fitness vacation
- ❑ work as a major league baseball scout
- ❑ travel to Vietnam
- ❑ ....
- ❑ ....
- ❑ ....
- ❑ ....

- ❏ be able to recite all of Oscar Wilde's
  The Ballad of Reading Gaol
- ❏ taste something new
- ❏ throw away my watch
- ❏ pick the five places on earth I most want to
  go to and make sure I get to them before
  I die
- ❏ see the Knicks win it all
- ❏ eat Limburger cheese in Limburg, Belgium
- ❏ be serenaded by a gypsy violinist
- ❏ eat a jalapeño pepper all by itself
- ❏ travel to America's newest national park—
  on three islands of American Samoa in
  the Pacific
- ❏ toast a friend at a birthday celebration
- ❏ see skateboarding become an Olympic
  sport
- ❏ mountain-bike Rollins Pass, Colorado, on
  the former railroad bed of the Denver
  Northwestern & Pacific Railway
- ❏ ....
- ❏ ....

❑ ....

❑ ....

❑ ....

❑ attend the Whitney Bienniale art exhibit

❑ learn to play the clarinet

❑ drive a Mercedes on the German autobahn

❑ do as in the *Rubaiyat* and picnic with "a loaf of bread beneath the bough, a flask of wine, a book of verse—and thou"

❑ tour the Baja in Mexico

❑ join the foreign correspondents for a drink on the veranda of the Norfolk Hotel in Nairobi, Kenya

❑ have Luciano Pavarotti sing "Una Furtiva Lagrima" just for me

❑ walk right through a door labeled "Private"

❑ print my Christmas cards from a woodcut of my own design

❑ see Napoleon's Tomb at Les Invalides in Paris

❑ use Pelé's famous moves to make a soccer goal

- ❏ become an adventure-travel outfitter
- ❏ cook on an open hearth
- ❏ ....
- ❏ ....
- ❏ ....
- ❏ start a community quilt project to raise money for a good cause
- ❏ samba in São Paulo
- ❏ hold a family reunion and meet all my living relatives
- ❏ convert to geothermal energy
- ❏ make love under the stars
- ❏ scuba dive a shipwreck off Anegada in the British Virgin Islands
- ❏ have adversaries, not enemies
- ❏ learn to play the guitar
- ❏ remember to back up the hard disk once a week
- ❏ reorganize my Rolodex
- ❏ admit that I like Spam
- ❏ hire a chauffeur for a wine-tasting tour of California's Napa Valley

❑ become a movie reviewer

❑ cycle around Lake Constance

❑ memorize the name of every country
    and be able to spot them on a map of
    the world

❑ install a practice squash court in my home

❑ live and work on a kibbutz for a month

❑ find out how much the Leaning Tower of
    Pisa leans

❑ win the yellow jersey in the Tour de France

❑ shop and dine underground in Toronto's
    sub sidewalk city

❑ ....

❑ ....

❑ ....

❑ drink a Pilsner beer in Wenceslas Square
    in Prague

❑ be part of the gallery at the Masters
    Tournament

❑ cruise the Mediterranean on one of the tall
    ships

❑ open a B&B in New Mexico

- ☐ make up a new Jelly Belly flavor
- ☐ see how jelly beans are made
- ☐ hunt with a bow and arrow
- ☐ accept that life is neither a bowl of cherries nor a mess of porridge
- ☐ win a batting championship
- ☐ ....
- ☐ ....
- ☐ ....
- ☐ ....
- ☐ cover a war as a reporter
- ☐ sell all my furniture at auction and start over again
- ☐ avoid middle-age spread
- ☐ cross the Pacific in a raft
- ☐ make a solo transatlantic flight
- ☐ run a major television network
- ☐ become a self-made millionaire
- ☐ work a foot-treadle sewing machine, just like my grandmother did
- ☐ drive a concept car
- ☐ go back and relearn geometry

- ❑ trek Africa from coast to coast
- ❑ comfort someone afflicted with sorrow
- ❑ bathe in a marble tub
- ❑ be named to the best-dressed list
- ❑ make my Carnegie Hall debut
- ❑ fly into the stratosphere
- ❑ stay at the historic King David Hotel
  in Jerusalem
- ❑ be a state legislator
- ❑ face reality
- ❑ give a day's work for a day's pay
- ❑ taste anchovies
- ❑ find the suitcase key without searching
- ❑ attend a thousand-dollar-a-plate dinner
- ❑ do a jazz tour of Chicago, New Orleans,
  and Memphis
- ❑ guest star on *Seinfeld* as Newman's sibling
- ❑ install a pull-chain toilet
- ❑ find a message in a bottle floating in
  the ocean
- ❑ put myself in somebody else's shoes
- ❑ learn to dance a Balanchine ballet

- ❑ ....
- ❑ ....
- ❑ be called an ace
- ❑ work as a Wall Street broker during a bull market
- ❑ celebrate Oktoberfest in Bavaria
- ❑ ride a steam train
- ❑ drink chilled champagne from a crystal glass on the roof of the World Trade Center
- ❑ coach football
- ❑ visualize what I want
- ❑ cycle through the "flowered towns" along the Summit Route of the Vosges Mountains in France
- ❑ visit Hoosier National Forest, Indiana
- ❑ produce a Broadway show
- ❑ wear a watch chain and fob
- ❑ dine under date palms in the garden of the Mamounia hotel in Marrakesh
- ❑ found a news-and-opinion magazine
- ❑ go on a spiritual retreat

- ❑ attend a debutante ball
- ❑ live within my means
- ❑ own an automobile with running boards
- ❑ keep a list of all the books I read, with quotes of my favorite passages
- ❑ finish an all-day sucker
- ❑ find a thousand dollars in a taxicab
- ❑ train horses
- ❑ ignore people who try to discourage me
- ❑ head a chain of stores
- ❑ design handbags for Gucci
- ❑ fix up and refinish an old rolltop desk
- ❑ run for Governor
- ❑ learn how to play euchre—and how not to be euchred
- ❑ make fresh cinnamon rolls for breakfast
- ❑ teach in a one-room schoolhouse
- ❑ raise my pain threshold
- ❑ ....
- ❑ ....
- ❑ ....

- ❑ set my hair in curlers
- ❑ welcome the return of double-decker buses to Fifth Avenue
- ❑ ....
- ❑ ....
- ❑ cycle through Portugal
- ❑ practice prudence
- ❑ hire a Lear jet and fly my date to the movies in another state
- ❑ make a shell necklace
- ❑ join the annual walk around the shoreline of Manhattan island
- ❑ win the weekly quiz and be on the air for the Sunday puzzle segment on NPR's *Weekend Edition*
- ❑ dress exclusively in Ralph Lauren's Polo fashions
- ❑ own a bulldog and name him Churchill
- ❑ go to a game at Yankee Stadium
- ❑ prepay my mortgage
- ❑ climb Brunelleschi's double dome on the cathedral of Florence, Italy

- ❑ lose my insecurities
- ❑ spend part of Christmas serving at a soup kitchen
- ❑ hook a rug
- ❑ sail among icebergs
- ❑ dance to the big band sound
- ❑ live to see the discovery of life on another planet
- ❑ find the cure for Parkinson's disease
- ❑ become director of a small, local museum
- ❑ avoid extremes
- ❑ sight Elvis
- ❑ learn the secret recipes of a great chef
- ❑ unpack my resentments and just enjoy myself
- ❑ have a platinum hit
- ❑ buy a thousand-dollar dress on impulse
- ❑ play a foot-pump organ
- ❑ ....
- ❑ ....
- ❑ ....
- ❑ ....

- ❏ visit "wicked Alexandria" in Egypt
- ❏ walk Edinburgh's Royal Mile
- ❏ get a tattoo removed
- ❏ become a travel guide, so I get to see all the places I've longed to visit
- ❏ walk my pug down Madison Avenue
- ❏ swim the anchor leg in a relay race and pull off a come-from-behind victory
- ❏ put my address book on computer
- ❏ understand the other person's point of view
- ❏ wear a wild-print Hawaiian shirt

- ❏ drink fresh water processed from saltwater
- ❏ spend a vacation living in a thatched cottage in a village in Great Britain
- ❏ stand up for a friend in trouble
- ❏ resist sexual temptation
- ❏ yield to sexual temptation
- ❏ ....
- ❏ ....

- ❑ live through a typhoon on a small Pacific island
- ❑ design museum exhibits
- ❑ attend a major auction at Sotheby's or Christie's in New York—and watch a bidding war
- ❑ wear a wig
- ❑ ....
- ❑ ....
- ❑ ....
- ❑ ....
- ❑ take a train to the top of Copacabana in Rio de Janeiro
- ❑ complete a 50-mile hike
- ❑ dress as Batman on Halloween
- ❑ decorate my dinnerware by painting scenes from my life on the plates
- ❑ learn Esperanto
- ❑ own a videophone
- ❑ expose a great hoax or forgery—like the Piltdown Man
- ❑ take up belly dancing

- ❏ ....
- ❏ ....
- ❏ ride a hydrofoil across the Bay of Naples
- ❏ use finger bowls at dinner
- ❏ make friends with people who manage to accomplish a lot
- ❏ consult an oracle
- ❏ find a mistake in a dictionary
- ❏ play bongos at 4 A.M. in a smoky Paris nightclub
- ❏ grow a beard
- ❏ lie on a beach in Goa, on India's Malabar Coast
- ❏ sit on a flagpole
- ❏ devise a fallback position in case Plan A fails
- ❏ become a sharpshooter
- ❏ undergo hypnosis in order to quit smoking
- ❏ paint my house a metallic blue trimmed in bright yellow
- ❏ get a George Clooney haircut
- ❏ attend the auto show

- ❏ visit Nan Madol, the ancient royal head-quarters on the island of Ponape in the Pacific
- ❏ vote via computer
- ❏ live in a villa on Capri
- ❏ make sure my will is in order and up to date—to save my heirs confusion or squabbling
- ❏ find a cure for baldness
- ❏ eat several small meals throughout the day instead of three big ones
- ❏ become a power broker
- ❏ swim in Reykjavik's outdoor (heated) pool in winter
- ❏ swallow a goldfish on behalf of a good cause
- ❏ own a voice-controlled computer
- ❏ go to a game at Fenway Park in Boston
- ❏ live in a fiberglass house
- ❏ ....
- ❏ ....
- ❏ ....

- ❑ choose what's right over what's expedient
- ❑ get a programmable coffee-making machine
- ❑ travel at 5,000 miles per hour
- ❑ pay attention to what is left unspoken in a relationship
- ❑ have calling cards
- ❑ own something once owned by John F. Kennedy
- ❑ participate in a Hawaiian luau
- ❑ volunteer for the dunk tank at the Memorial Day festival
- ❑ be able to read tea leaves
- ❑ accept the blame when I deserve it
- ❑ see lightning strike twice in the same place
- ❑ volunteer for overnight duty at the home-less shelter
- ❑ travel the Great Lakes
- ❑ ....
- ❑ ....
- ❑ go to bed when I'm tired
- ❑ join the volunteer fire department

- ❑ shear a sheep
- ❑ have a suit custom made by a Savile Row tailor
- ❑ get a new brother or sister
- ❑ overcome my fear of heights by climbing a mountain
- ❑ ....
- ❑ ....
- ❑ ....
- ❑ ....
- ❑ swim the Bosporous
- ❑ own a chain saw
- ❑ embrace change in society and in my life
- ❑ give up makeup
- ❑ peer into the crater of Mount Vesuvius
- ❑ play with a cornhusk doll
- ❑ own a frost-free refrigerator
- ❑ discover a way to dissipate hurricanes and tornadoes before they can cause harm
- ❑ portage a canoe
- ❑ write children's books
- ❑ hear a concert by Yo-Yo Ma

- ❏ wear a wrist radio
- ❏ find an ancient papyrus scroll in the caves of Egypt
- ❏ play Dizzy Gillespie's trumpet

- ❏ crochet an afghan
- ❏ maintain a healthy sex drive
- ❏ stop biting my nails
- ❏ campaign for universal, subsidized higher education
- ❏ take in the lumberjack world championship competition in Wisconsin
- ❏ pay off a loan in half the time
- ❏ learn by osmosis in my sleep
- ❏ develop a beautifully modulated speaking voice
- ❏ sail around the island of Manhattan
- ❏ ....
- ❏ ....
- ❏ ....
- ❏ ....
- ❏ live to see the development of no-crash airplanes

- ❑ become a Washington lobbyist
- ❑ eat a breakfast of banana doughnuts and black coffee
- ❑ be sustained by an inner strength
- ❑ eat Rice-A-Roni in San Francisco
- ❑ ask Rush Limbaugh to lower his voice
- ❑ keep my promises
- ❑ spend a winter in an Inuit village in Canada's Northwest Territories
- ❑ paint a self-portrait
- ❑ be on the set for the making of a movie from start to finish
- ❑ practice loyalty
- ❑ attend a Japanese tea ceremony
- ❑ score a baseball game
- ❑ fight a duel—and win
- ❑ live to see human underwater settlements
- ❑ earn double my salary
- ❑ meet a person with a transplanted heart
- ❑ join the Marines
- ❑ take the tram up St. Louis's Gateway Arch
- ❑ own a Tiffany lamp

- ❏ slow-dance with my lover to old '50s records
- ❏ ....
- ❏ ....
- ❏ ....
- ❏ be able to file my taxes electronically
- ❏ have a wallet full of new bills
- ❏ ride a Caterpillar tractor
- ❏ share credit
- ❏ excavate a dolmen in Great Britain
- ❏ ride in an armored tank
- ❏ walk down New York's Great White Way
- ❏ see a desert made fertile
- ❏ celebrate Easter at a sunrise service in the Rockies
- ❏ drive a motorboat
- ❏ endow a scholarship
- ❏ work at a drive-in restaurant
- ❏ create a landscape of ornamental grasses
- ❏ own a Dior original
- ❏ kiss again the person who gave me my first kiss

- ❑ plant a gingko tree in the city
- ❑ volunteer to work in a hospice
- ❑ visit Battle Creek and see my breakfast cereal being made
- ❑ go back in time and be in the audience for the opening night of *West Side Story*
- ❑ waste nothing
- ❑ see how maps are made from satellite photos
- ❑ understand fractals
- ❑ win public office and make good on my promises
- ❑ ....
- ❑ ....
- ❑ ....
- ❑ watch a magazine being printed
- ❑ ride a burro in Mexico
- ❑ realize my capacity for original thinking
- ❑ wear an old Etonian tie
- ❑ sneak onto and jump off a train boxcar
- ❑ attend a game in the Carrier Dome
- ❑ become a longshoreman

- ❑ visit the Renaissance gardens of Villa Lante
  in Bagnaia, near Viterbo, Italy
- ❑ expose a spy
- ❑ mine for gold in the Klondike
- ❑ head a charitable organization
- ❑ possess the seven virtues, avoid the seven
  deadly sins
- ❑ throw a bon voyage party aboard ship
  before I sail
- ❑ flirt with Paul Newman
- ❑ see my own motorcycle being built
  at the Harley-Davidson plant
  in Wisconsin
- ❑ be able to sleep on an airplane
- ❑ drive to the office in a Rolls-Royce
- ❑ attend avant-garde theater
- ❑ observe a tsunami—from a safe distance
- ❑ be the subject of a flurry of newspaper
  publicity
- ❑ ....
- ❑ ....
- ❑ ....

- ❏ commission a coat of arms
- ❏ own a corgi
- ❏ stroll hand-in-hand with my lover down the Champs Elysées
- ❏ breed racehorses
- ❏ install gold fittings in my bathroom
- ❏ ....
- ❏ ....
- ❏ have my hair done at home
- ❏ be paged in the lobby of Claridge's Hotel in London
- ❏ ride in a mine elevator
- ❏ invent the jam-free slide projector
- ❏ do no harm
- ❏ debate with proponents of both far-right and far-left ideologies
- ❏ find my exact double
- ❏ pledge a significant contribution to my local National Public Radio station
- ❏ start a fish hatchery
- ❏ tend those who are sick in body or at heart

- ❏ be naughty
- ❏ have pizza delivered to my employees whenever they work late
- ❏ endow an award for utilitarian design
- ❏ gamble casually for high stakes
- ❏ expose the foibles of the jet set in a block-buster novel
- ❏ solve a mystery
- ❏ remain unperturbed by the unavoidable
- ❏ get a vaccination with a needleless syringe
- ❏ ....
- ❏ ....
- ❏ ....
- ❏ build an elaborate mausoleum
- ❏ have access to a skybox at the stadium
- ❏ stay at the Gleneagles in Perthshire, Scotland, and play The Monarch's championship golf course
- ❏ drive a Good Humor truck
- ❏ collect potted succulent plants
- ❏ throw a lavish celebrity party that will be talked of for years to come

- ❑ own a ranch in Wyoming
- ❑ have John Mellencamp play a private concert in my backyard
- ❑ give someone a compliment
- ❑ dine at the most expensive restaurant in Los Angeles
- ❑ play polo
- ❑ own a typewriter, a vestige of a bygone era
- ❑ explore the Dolomite Alps in Italy
- ❑ discover a cure for hay fever
- ❑ observe the moons of Jupiter through a telescope
- ❑ live in a houseboat on the Thames in London
- ❑ be asked to compile a guide to the best cheeseburgers in America
- ❑ become a chess grandmaster
- ❑ live by the lunar calendar
- ❑ ....
- ❑ ....
- ❑ ....
- ❑ ....

❑ ....
❑ make the cover of *Paris-Match* magazine
❑ taste a mooseburger in Alaska
❑ grow orchids
❑ create and stock my own backyard pond
❑ be offered a listing in the Social Register—
   and turn it down
❑ make a lavender basket with a grapevine
   handle
❑ bring doughnuts and hot coffee to workers
   shoveling snow on a cold morning
❑ ride in my private railroad car
❑ sit ringside at a cabaret performance
❑ be listed in *Who's Who*
❑ hit high C
❑ harvest cloves on the island of Zanzibar
❑ watch a lobster molt
❑ spend a year being "irresponsible,"
   because if I don't, I'll always regret it
❑ carefully drop a name and have it work
❑ memorize a poem by Walt Whitman
❑ operate a summer theater

- ❑ be a witty, sparkling conversationalist
- ❑ bicycle Prince Edward Island
- ❑ set my sights higher
- ❑ teach ballroom dancing to young children
- ❑ master sewing
- ❑ bake almond croissants
- ❑ own a vintage Cadillac—with fins
- ❑ live in an adobe house with Navajo rugs and hanging red peppers
- ❑ sow a garden with heirloom seeds
- ❑ contribute money and goods to feed the hungry
- ❑ welcome the neighbors to an open house in my new home
- ❑ take good care of my repair equipment
- ❑ ....
- ❑ ....
- ❑ ....
- ❑ ....
- ❑ fish for cabezon in the Strait of Juan de Fuca, off the coast of Washington State
- ❑ be a guest at Buckingham Palace

- ❑ live without Velcro
- ❑ celebrate National Hamburger & Pickle Month with hamburgers and pickles
- ❑ observe a voodoo ritual in Haiti
- ❑ figure out what went on in the ancient Greek mystery rituals at Eleusis
- ❑ graduate from high school
- ❑ eat till I'm satisfied—not a bite more
- ❑ ask the *I Ching* for advice
- ❑ win on the last throw of the dice
- ❑ keep a telescope beside the bedroom window
- ❑ make my own perfume
- ❑ ride the fabled Moscow subway system
- ❑ get a phone call from my child "just to say I love you"
- ❑ ask all the right questions
- ❑ tour behind the scenes at Universal City in California
- ❑ ....
- ❑ ....
- ❑ ....

❏ bodysurf in Arizona's man-made ocean
❏ visit a drive-through safari park
❏ take my dreams seriously
❏ own an Arabian mare
❏ set type on an old handpress
❏ be a multilingual interpreter
❏ catch the bride's bouquet
❏ install a dumbwaiter
❏ have Thanksgiving dinner for breakfast, as
    the Pilgrims did
❏ ....
❏ ....
❏ steal home
❏ visit the elephant-shaped house in
    Margate, New Jersey
❏ participate in a cattle roundup and help
    brand an animal
❏ ride the Scream Machine at Six Flags
❏ own an electric carving knife
❏ make up a great CB "handle"
❏ untie my emotional knots
❏ make *Law Review*

❑ persuade the airlines that safety is more
    important than food service
❑ make advertisers pay *me* to look at
    their ads
❑ create a terrarium
❑ come back in a thousand years to see what
    people in the year 3000 think of us
❑ learn Portuguese
❑ take apart a telephone to see how it works
❑ ....
❑ ....
❑ ....
❑ ....
❑ be surrounded by winners
❑ own a 1952 Harley-Davidson "FatBoy"
❑ experience a sense of belonging
❑ work in the city, live in the mountains
❑ play PacMan
❑ throw a 1950s dance party
❑ build an underground house
❑ be served breakfast in bed with a rose and
    the newspaper

- ❏ fly a cargo plane
- ❏ ....
- ❏ ....
- ❏ ....
- ❏ dress in Gulf War desert fatigues
- ❏ bungee-jump off the Eiffel Tower
- ❏ save the Chesapeake
- ❏ put away enough money to retire whenever I want to
- ❏ go back in time to share an evening of epigrams with Oscar Wilde
- ❏ become a court stenographer
- ❏ guest star on *The Muppet Show*
- ❏ see an alligator in the wild from a safe distance
- ❏ shoot with a longbow
- ❏ find out how pop-up toasters work
- ❏ have thin thighs
- ❏ play the cello
- ❏ drive across the southern tier of Canada
- ❏ read all of William Faulkner's works
- ❏ learn to play a saw as a musical instrument

- ❑ rent a French farmhouse for the summer
- ❑ retrace Darwin's voyage on the *Beagle*
- ❑ own shares in a condo
- ❑ raise holstein dairy cows
- ❑ spend a month reading history
- ❑ roll in the mud
- ❑ find my own private island
- ❑ study geology and know the features of my native topography
- ❑ drink right out of Evian's spring
- ❑ start a local historical society
- ❑ ....
- ❑ ....
- ❑ ....
- ❑ ....
- ❑ decide what I want to be when I grow up
- ❑ travel to Worms, where Martin Luther made his stand
- ❑ experience childbirth
- ❑ find a quiet pool in a gurgling stream and fish all day long by myself
- ❑ announce major league baseball

- ❑ soar to show business stardom
- ❑ radically change my profession—without going back to school
- ❑ take a jazz exercize class
- ❑ become a bicoastal celebrity
- ❑ see Lake Ladoga, the sole lifeline during the Siege of Leningrad in World War II
- ❑ try patience instead of giving an order
- ❑ be sought after as a weekend guest at friends' country houses
- ❑ combine all my interests into one goal
- ❑ volunteer at a zoo
- ❑ hike the Andes
- ❑ see a recipe of mine published in the newspaper
- ❑ stop rationalizing
- ❑ encourage my children to celebrate their own uniqueness
- ❑ own an appliance that outlasts its warranty
- ❑ shatter the glass ceiling
- ❑ take a first-class cruise around the world

- ❑ never have to worry about cholesterol
- ❑ ride a motor scooter
- ❑ eat cannoli on the streets of Little Italy
- ❑ swim in the lagoon of Rangiroa
- ❑ be fluent in pig Latin
- ❑ employ a butler
- ❑ convert a school bus into my own mobile home
- ❑ see Olduvai Gorge in Tanzania, where the first hominids walked
- ❑ experience virtual reality
- ❑ ride on FDR's presidential yacht, the *Potomac*, out of Oakland, California
- ❑ be a Renaissance person
- ❑ live in a high-rise on Chicago's Lake Shore Drive
- ❑ attend a private screening in Hollywood
- ❑ own a bright red barn
- ❑ not sweat the small stuff
- ❑ go behind the scenes and watch theater costumes being made
- ❑ travel to Java

- ❑ stow away on a nuclear submarine
- ❑ ....
- ❑ ....
- ❑ ....
- ❑ ....
- ❑ work as a stablehand in the Kentucky bluegrass country
- ❑ become a lexicographer
- ❑ walk ten blocks to work
- ❑ lead tours of the great castles of Europe
- ❑ start my own business
- ❑ defy conventional wisdom
- ❑ live in a culturally lively city or town
- ❑ be named one of *Time* magazine's "New Millionaires"
- ❑ sail through the Suez Canal
- ❑ open a bookstore in a small town in the mountains
- ❑ sleep out under the stars in Death Valley
- ❑ journey to the center of my self through guided meditation

- ❏ ....
- ❏ set the table with paper place mats for the children to draw on
- ❏ learn what the animal world has to teach
- ❏ read *The Iliad*
- ❏ make a habit of walking upstairs backwards for exercise
- ❏ learn to make Popsicles
- ❏ slip some wild and crazy adventure into my daily life
- ❏ do my hair in dreadlocks
- ❏ collect comic books
- ❏ paint an outdoor scene on the side of my car
- ❏ own and operate a whole-grain bakery
- ❏ bike the 400-series trails of Crested Butte, Colorado
- ❏ start composting
- ❏ fly down to Rio
- ❏ throw away the scales
- ❏ learn one great card trick
- ❏ interview a world leader

- ❑ interview the "man in the street"
- ❑ memorize Martin Luther King's "I Have a Dream" speech
- ❑ stock my kitchen with professional cookware from E. Dehillerin in Paris
- ❑ see the Dome of the Rock, the great Muslim shrine in Jerusalem
- ❑ ....
- ❑ ....
- ❑ visit all the towns in the United States named Springfield
- ❑ be rich enough to sponsor an elementary class through college
- ❑ become a political commentator
- ❑ pilot a rescue helicopter
- ❑ go skydiving over Monument Valley
- ❑ become a judge
- ❑ see a grizzly bear catch a Chinook salmon
- ❑ visit Fort McHenry in Baltimore, which is commemorated in the "Star-Spangled Banner"
- ❑ learn orienteering

- ❏ have a loving relationship with my spouse
- ❏ understand there may be no such thing as a perfect relationship
- ❏ stay out of my own way
- ❏ find a cure for ALS, Lou Gehrig's disease
- ❏ harvest Chesapeake oysters off a skipjack
- ❏ own a leafblower
- ❏ keep a record of the lessons I learn
- ❏ see my book selected for Oprah Winfrey's Book Club
- ❏ become a building contractor
- ❏ roller skate across the Golden Gate Bridge
- ❏ see the room where Keats died beside the Spanish Steps in Rome
- ❏ ....
- ❏ live with all wicker furniture
- ❏ aim for success, not perfection
- ❏ shop for groceries just once a week
- ❏ figure out where my talents lie and work to fulfill them
- ❏ see a repair person show up on time and fix what's wrong in no time

- ❑ ....
- ❑ pitch a no-hitter
- ❑ have the build to be a jockey
- ❑ be able to jump up and click my heels together in the air
- ❑ give big applause to small achievements
- ❑ undertake a challenge of epic proportions
- ❑ have a two-line telephone
- ❑ ....
- ❑ ....
- ❑ ....
- ❑ ....
- ❑ ....
- ❑ see the fall colors in Brown County State Park
- ❑ taste reindeer in Finland
- ❑ try to accept a situation *before* I try to change it
- ❑ install a two-way pet door
- ❑ watch a kickboxing match in Thailand
- ❑ grow lettuce hydroponically
- ❑ have a loving relationship with my children

- ❑ see the rhododendrons bloom in the springtime in Nepal
- ❑ have Michelangelo give me a tattoo
- ❑ turn one room of the house into a solarium
- ❑ campaign against strip-mining
- ❑ work off my cellulite
- ❑ win the jackpot from a one-armed bandit in Atlantic City
- ❑ think hard before I cross a picket line
- ❑ travel to Timbuktu
- ❑ go down in the *Alvin* submarine on a deep-sea mission
- ❑ ....
- ❑ ....
- ❑ collect stamps
- ❑ start up and succeed at an Internet business
- ❑ sketch with pastel crayons
- ❑ retire overseas
- ❑ spend a month of solitude in an isolated woodland cabin
- ❑ see Mount Rushmore

- ❑ learn to dance flamenco
- ❑ help eliminate one cause of poverty—such as housing—in my town
- ❑ read the travel books written by those intrepid 19th-century British travelers
- ❑ ....
- ❑ ....
- ❑ ....
- ❑ have a spouse who still finds me surprising after many years of marriage
- ❑ clean out the refrigerator
- ❑ put money in any red-flag parking meters I pass on my daily walk
- ❑ perform the unexpected
- ❑ make a new friend of an old person
- ❑ sample Chubby Hubby ice cream at the Ben & Jerry's factory in Waterbury, Vermont
- ❑ visit the remaining Shaker communities
- ❑ have an out-of-body experience
- ❑ open my mail to find a free airline ticket to London

- ❏ live among energetic people
- ❏ study mime
- ❏ learn to cha-cha
- ❏ perform a spiritual inventory of my life
- ❏ report a slumlord to the authorities
- ❏ ....
- ❏ ....
- ❏ ....
- ❏ become an independent filmmaker
- ❏ run a petting zoo for small children
- ❏ work at a big desk facing a picture window, viewing endless mesas and big sky
- ❏ have a lifetime supply of Tootsie Rolls
- ❏ keep an airplane in a small hangar behind the house
- ❏ have a place for everything and keep everything in its place
- ❏ teach Sunday school
- ❏ put a bay leaf under my pillow to see if it brings sweet dreams
- ❏ cycle through New York state's Finger Lakes region

❑ eliminate deadlines and still get the
  job done
❑ be 6' 2" and have a full head of hair
❑ receive mail from all over the world
❑ take a course in assertiveness training
❑ go to a toga party
❑ throw a pie in someone's face
❑ live alone
❑ see the Muppets in person
❑ cruise from Bergen to Kirkenes on a
  Norwegian mailboat
❑ become the female Johnny Carson
❑ own my own Vermont Teddy Bear
❑ order pizza on the Web
❑ have enough confidence in myself to ask
  for help
❑ follow a FedEx package to see just how it
  gets where it's going
❑ be considered an original
❑ ....
❑ ....
❑ ....

- ❑ get a pedicure
- ❑ blow the world's largest gum bubble
- ❑ have fresh roses on the table all
  summer long
- ❑ own a set of fine copper cookware
- ❑ show respect, not reverence, for my elders
- ❑ be careful what I promise
- ❑ budget my time as if it were money
- ❑ eschew discouragement
- ❑ keep a record of gifts I give to avoid giving
  the same thing again
- ❑ discipline my thinking to keep the focus on
  the problem
- ❑ see the homecoming of all
  Vietnam MIAs
- ❑ fit into my wedding dress again
- ❑ collect quartz and display it in natural light
- ❑ ....
- ❑ ....
- ❑ leave a legacy of good feelings
- ❑ learn how to pick my fights
- ❑ win the fights I pick

- ❑ tour the ruins of an abbey on a windswept island off Scotland
- ❑ ....
- ❑ ....
- ❑ ....
- ❑ escape from a sinking ship
- ❑ enjoy the fruits of my labor
- ❑ list the contents on the side of every storage box in the garage
- ❑ travel to Khartoum, in the Sudan
- ❑ sort my books alphabetically by subject
- ❑ earn the respect of my employer
- ❑ earn the respect of my colleagues
- ❑ be a princess for a day
- ❑ do for my homemade potato chips what Paul Newman did for popcorn
- ❑ curb my hardheadedness
- ❑ enjoy a domestic life without discord
- ❑ escape serious disaster
- ❑ dress in period costume to re-enact Colonial life at Old Sturbridge Village
- ❑ go to an oxygen bar in Tokyo

- ❏ inherit a house in the rolling hills of
  Virginia
- ❏ complete all the tasks on my daily to-do list
- ❏ paint a masterpiece
- ❏ wander through the unblemished rain
  forest of Dominica, in the Caribbean
- ❏ give my children both roots and wings
- ❏ eradicate meanness
- ❏ graduate from college
- ❏ give time and money to
  help save Long Island Sound
- ❏ have my love requited
- ❏ design and plant a garden that attracts
  butterflies
- ❏ walk across the Sahara from north to south
- ❏ live in a monastery
- ❏ control my actions with my will
- ❏ gain powerful allies
- ❏ ....
- ❏ ....
- ❏ ....
- ❏ ....

- ❑ grow African violets
- ❑ taste cranberry ketchup
- ❑ cultivate a love for home life
- ❑ have a friend who serves as the sibling I never had
- ❑ learn to play croquet
- ❑ design a safe car
- ❑ learn which bridges to cross and which to burn
- ❑ serve as school principal for a day
- ❑ ....
- ❑ ....
- ❑ ....
- ❑ master my personal computer
- ❑ at 90, have the mind and body of a 50-year-old
- ❑ live flamboyantly
- ❑ go to a cigar bar
- ❑ live off the dividends from my blue chip stocks
- ❑ get the fate I deserve
- ❑ restore art

❑ ....

❑ ....

❑ ....

❑ learn to cook genuine Southern
   fried chicken

❑ do original work

❑ own the local television station

❑ visit the Dionne Quintuplets Museum
   in Canada

❑ work with an herbalist to prevent disease

❑ swim underwater the length of an
   Olympic-size pool

❑ learn biofeedback

❑ rescue a friend from misfortune

❑ keep a baby rhinoceros as a pet

❑ be easily contented

❑ win out over an opponent

❑ keep my eyesight sharp enough that I
   don't need bifocals

❑ have my own one-person art exhibit

❑ type 60 words a minute

❑ learn to be invisible

314

- ❑ take the mineral baths at the historic Greenbrier Hotel in White Sulphur Springs, West Virginia
- ❑ signal summer by hanging fuchsia on the deck
- ❑ indulge in a seaweed wrap at a spa
- ❑ learn Yiddish
- ❑ be in England for Guy Fawkes' Day
- ❑ ride in a surrey with fringe on top
- ❑ ....
- ❑ ....
- ❑ ....
- ❑ organize my closet by category and color
- ❑ operate a tack shop
- ❑ own a solid-gold toothpick
- ❑ make the winning touchdown in the Super Bowl
- ❑ be a haberdasher
- ❑ make a film about the Brontë family
- ❑ star in my own television show
- ❑ have x-ray vision
- ❑ invent the all-week sucker

- ❏ write a book that changes someone's life for the better
- ❏ meet the inventor of Post-its
- ❏ be a contender
- ❏ strive for moderation in all things
- ❏ train a falcon to hunt
- ❏ relax and be sloppy
- ❏ ski down the Matterhorn
- ❏ sell my *Star Trek* memorabilia
- ❏ get up an hour before the rest of the family to enjoy private time
- ❏ prevent osteoporosis
- ❏ stretch my paycheck so I regularly put money in my savings account
- ❏ be able to accept help in time of need
- ❏ win at bingo
- ❏ let go of distractions
- ❏ photograph the Rockies by moonlight
- ❏ eat, drink, and be merry
- ❏ know how to clean anything
- ❏ ....
- ❏ ....

❑ ....

❑ ....

❑ ....

❑ ....

❑ declare a double major in college

❑ lie on a bed of nails

❑ sail the Chesapeake Bay and fish for crab

❑ be aware of grammar when I speak
    and write

❑ have a hairdresser who never says a word

❑ paint pottery

❑ write my living will

❑ play a command performance

❑ observe Easter on the island of Mykonos

❑ buy stock at the bottom of the market

❑ give away all my clothes and buy a
    whole new wardrobe

❑ trade in my faults for virtues

❑ be a gondolier

❑ get a gift certificate for a week at a
    luxury resort

❑ throw a haunted-house party

317

- ❏ not have to referee my children
- ❏ collect art
- ❏ leave the world a little better than I found it
- ❏ give out fruit instead of candy at Halloween
- ❏ remember names
- ❏ find a reliable baby-sitter
- ❏ act with enthusiasm
- ❏ discover that I have a talent for mathematics
- ❏ party with the beautiful people
- ❏ help achieve racial harmony
- ❏ see a seven-man pyramid on the high wire
- ❏ paint my car salmon-colored
- ❏ outfit myself at the thrift shop
- ❏ be self-sufficient
- ❏ maintain a solid bank balance
- ❏ touch a great painting
- ❏ represent the U.S. in treaty negotiations
- ❏ be considered fun
- ❏ play in a kitchen rhythm band
- ❏ ....
- ❏ ....

❑ ....

❑ ....

❑ fulfill my potential as a person, spouse,
   and parent

❑ practice neatness

❑ read all of Saint-Exupéry's writings

❑ collect PEZ candy dispensers

❑ have only the insurance I need

❑ talk to Yoko Ono about John Lennon

❑ donate a tree to the local park

❑ become a fire-eating trial lawyer

❑ learn stone masonry

❑ participate in the Blessing of the Fishing
   Fleet in Provincetown, Massachusetts

❑ lead a life of adventure

❑ travel to Afghanistan

❑ own only no-iron clothes

❑ bake bread with a variety of flours

❑ reorganize my entire house

❑ import a racing Porsche

❑ uphold standards of intellectual rigor

❑ search for an out-of-print book until I find it

- ❏ ....
- ❏ ....
- ❏ ....
- ❏ stroll a beach on each of the six continents
- ❏ beat a professional in golf
- ❏ join a get-rich-slowly scheme
- ❏ tour the Chequamegon National Forest in northern Wisconsin
- ❏ keep a humidifier in my house to stave off dryness in plants and people
- ❏ alter my clothes myself
- ❏ grow a fruit tree from seed
- ❏ see my pet perform in a movie
- ❏ invest via computer
- ❏ win a glorious triumph
- ❏ have the sense of being in charge
- ❏ rent an art masterpiece to hang in the living room
- ❏ sail around the world in the "roaring twenties" latitude at top speed
- ❏ avoid responsibility until middle age
- ❏ hear the bells of Notre Dame

❑ dare great things

❑ ride a horse along the wide beaches of
  Cape Cod

❑ find the answer to the question "Which
  came first, the chicken or the egg?"

❑ ride in a golf cart

❑ picnic on an empty beach on an island in
  the South Pacific

❑ laugh often and hard

❑ make life an experiment

❑ throw the switch that opens Grand Coulee
  Dam for a scheduled release

❑ ....

❑ ....

❑ ....

❑ perfect the equation of water and rice
  so I don't keep burning the bottoms of
  my pots

❑ visit Storm King Center, the outdoor
  sculpture museum at West Point

❑ put my marriage first

❑ learn to be a pastry chef

❑ ....

❑ ....

❑ dive down in a submersible for a close-up
   look at the *Titanic*

❑ experience ecstasy (not the drug)

❑ attend a Cabinet meeting

❑ see Angel Falls in Venezuela

❑ be a clown

❑ have high arches

❑ ski Mount Snow, Vermont

❑ follow all the advice for saving money on
   heat and electricity

❑ plan for my golden years

❑ turn my property into a
   bird preserve

❑ marshal my arguments in my mind before
   opening my mouth

❑ carpe diem—seize the day

❑ renovate a barn into a living space

❑ stop worrying

❑ upgrade my computer by myself

❑ be interviewed by a pollster

❏ observe the patterns of bird migration at
   Cape May, New Jersey
❏ get a digital phone answering machine
❏ grow my hair down to my waist
❏ see the Shroud of Turin
❏ cast my vote for a write-in candidate
❏ win an appointment to West Point
❏ play Jimi Hendrix's guitar
❏ enjoy sex more than money
❏ visit a tanning salon
❏ command a ship
❏ retrace the route of the Crusades
❏ become expert at croquet
❏ install a weather vane
❏ ....
❏ ....
❏ ....
❏ ....
❏ hit the grand slam that wins it when
   the team is down 3–0 in the bottom
   of the ninth
❏ climb Mount Fuji in Japan

- ❑ shoot the cannon in the *1812* Overture
- ❑ have a gold tooth
- ❑ spend a rainy weekend curled up with a book in front of the fire
- ❑ go back and visit the old neighborhood
- ❑ give up caffeine
- ❑ pay the highway toll for the car behind me
- ❑ learn to meditate for relaxation
- ❑ eat more vegetables, less meat
- ❑ cross the international date line
- ❑ learn Chinese
- ❑ own a rocking chair
- ❑ transcend my everyday routine at least once every day

- ❑ see my fifty-dollar vegetable garden yield hundreds of dollars worth of produce
- ❑ ....
- ❑ ....
- ❑ ....
- ❑ live in an ocean-view bungalow on a Caribbean island

- ❑ have a backyard backboard so I can practice tennis
- ❑ become a morning person
- ❑ tour the 17th-century fortress cities of France built by Vauban
- ❑ ....
- ❑ ....
- ❑ ....
- ❑ see wild mustangs
- ❑ vacation on Sardinia's Emerald Coast
- ❑ buy, restore, and live in an old windmill
- ❑ eat strawberries and cream at Wimbledon
- ❑ gather up all the loose change in the house—and buy something with it
- ❑ push my comfort level
- ❑ plant a garden full of four-leaf clovers
- ❑ participate in the grape harvest in Burgundy
- ❑ own a standing globe
- ❑ buy a zoo
- ❑ talk with the kids about sex without embarrassment

- ❏ be the unnamed source in a breakthrough newspaper exposé
- ❏ visit a working coffee plantation
- ❏ become a video producer
- ❏ see whooping cranes at Aransas National Wildlife Refuge in Texas
- ❏ reread J. D. Salinger's *Catcher in the Rye*
- ❏ go over Niagara Falls in a barrel
- ❏ ride in a horse-drawn sleigh
- ❏ become an entertainment journalist
- ❏ visit all the presidential libraries
- ❏ go skinny-dipping with a conservative
- ❏ take part in a market-research survey
- ❏ grow a prize pumpkin big enough to be Cinderella's coach
- ❏ experience a hair-raising airplane emergency—and live to tell of it
- ❏ sleep on Egyptian cotton sheets
- ❏ wear diamonds
- ❏ see a herd of elk
- ❏ fish in an Alaskan stream accessible only by airplane

- ❑ look sleek in bike pants
- ❑ attend a university lecture
- ❑ stand on the busiest corner in the world—
  59th Street and Lexington Avenue in
  New York City
- ❑ collect books for the local library
- ❑ win at badminton
- ❑ cruise the Argentine coast from north to
  south
- ❑ ....
- ❑ ....
- ❑ ....
- ❑ get my boss's job
- ❑ take a Dale Carnegie course
- ❑ make a sculpture out of Play-Doh
- ❑ find a doctor who still makes house calls
- ❑ be involved in counterintelligence
- ❑ hire a personal image consultant
- ❑ fly to Maui with my lover and count the
  grains of sand
- ❑ tour the gardens of Victoria, Canada
- ❑ cross the High Plains in a covered wagon

❏ design period sets for Hollywood

❏ ....

❏ ....

❏ form a band and play club dates
    on weekends

❏ throw a tantrum and get it out of my
    system

❏ design customized travel vacations

❏ take charge of my life

❏ tow a French gypsy cart behind a 1957
    Bentley convertible

❏ be a fly on the wall at the annual personnel
    review

❏ have my own amusement park in the
    backyard

❏ walk around Annapurna

❏ take joy in serving others

❏ carve the oarlocks for gondolas

❏ make life my classroom

❏ be the auctioneer for estate sales

❏ march in the oldest U.S. Independence
    Day parade in Bristol, Rhode Island

- ❑ spend my life as an archaeologist
- ❑ own a stable of racehorses
- ❑ approach old facts in new ways
- ❑ apprentice to a mule driver
- ❑ drive U.S. Route 50 in Nevada, "the Loneliest Road in America"
- ❑ practice strategic planning for life as well as for work
- ❑ make a successful business out of something I love doing
- ❑ weave a tapestry
- ❑ participate in Iowa's border-to-border Ragbrai bicycle ride
- ❑ fish for barramundi off Australia's west coast
- ❑ grow spiritually
- ❑ grow tropical hibiscus
- ❑ make my own cable-knit sweater
- ❑ attend a service in Washington's National Cathedral
- ❑ ....
- ❑ ....

- [ ] have an overseas phone conversation in a foreign language
- [ ] live without a schedule
- [ ] learn to spell
- [ ] pay my bills in cash
- [ ] go kite buggying
- [ ] use all my letters in Scrabble to make the word "quixotic" on a triple-word score
- [ ] have my sunglasses with me when I need them
- [ ] ....
- [ ] ....
- [ ] ....
- [ ] ....
- [ ] leave my mark
- [ ] visit Willie Wonka's chocolate factory
- [ ] catch a fly ball at the ballpark
- [ ] ride a Jet-ski
- [ ] own a Russian astrakhan hat
- [ ] become expert at making fires—in the fireplace and at the campsite
- [ ] write a biography of a great woman

- ❏ make the phone calls I dread making
- ❏ see the wolves in the wild in Yellowstone National Park
- ❏ reconcile two enemies
- ❏ ....
- ❏ ....
- ❏ travel to Ethiopia
- ❏ tame and train a wild horse
- ❏ try on a suit of mail
- ❏ vacation in a crofter's hut on the Scottish coast
- ❏ conduct a symphony orchestra
- ❏ play a Stradivarius violin
- ❏ tour the world looking for bumper car sites
- ❏ carve my own chess set
- ❏ be a fly on the wall at a publishing meeting where they decide what books to publish
- ❏ build my own wooden canoe
- ❏ view the Rhine from the top of the Cologne Cathedral
- ❏ get my family out the door to work and school on time

- ❑ win a patent
- ❑ assist in the birth of a baby
- ❑ taste escargots
- ❑ visit York Minster Cathedral in England
- ❑ help save the nation's sand dunes
- ❑ make a clay mask of my own face
- ❑ sleep alone in the forest
- ❑ ....
- ❑ ....
- ❑ get an all-in-one remote control for the TV, VCR, cable, and CD player
- ❑ redesign my vacuum cleaner to suit my precise needs
- ❑ raft the Snake River
- ❑ head to an all-night diner when I can't sleep
- ❑ read a book from cover to cover in one sitting
- ❑ learn how to index
- ❑ see my album cover at the Rock and Roll Hall of Fame—and not among the One Hit Wonders

- ❏ be a trader at the stock exchange
- ❏ treat myself to front-row seats at a Hootie and the Blowfish concert
- ❏ visit the grave of my hero
- ❏ practice Ayurveda, the ancient healing science of India
- ❏ find lost treasure in the bottom of my dresser drawers
- ❏ make M&M cookies
- ❏ break a taboo
- ❏ do shadow puppets
- ❏ shave my head
- ❏ get Toshiro Mifune's autograph
- ❏ upgrade to first class on a long flight
- ❏ not argue about money
- ❏ tour the medina of Fez, Morocco
- ❏ ....
- ❏ ....
- ❏ ....
- ❏ ....
- ❏ visit the Seven Natural Wonders of the World in one year

- ❏ stay awake for 24 hours straight
- ❏ see the island fox found only on the Channel Islands
- ❏ eat cotton candy—just like when I was a kid
- ❏ cross a line I haven't crossed before
- ❏ stop imagining different endings for books
- ❏ ask out a stranger on impulse
- ❏ be a cowboy
- ❏ watch the whales out of Provincetown
- ❏ wear an ascot
- ❏ get married on the top of a mountain—after climbing there
- ❏ e-mail the President
- ❏ hold a Jimmy Cagney movie festival
- ❏ ....
- ❏ ....
- ❏ ....
- ❏ climb Mount Lassen
- ❏ sneak into a sold-out show
- ❏ own a lifetime supply of Pilot Explorer pens
- ❏ write a comic novel

- ❏ photograph the Jeffrey Pine on Yosemite's Sentinel Dome
- ❏ get lost in the Ardennes Forest of Belgium
- ❏ ....
- ❏ ....
- ❏ pig out on Walker's shortbread
- ❏ watch spring arrive in the desert
- ❏ explore a tidal pool
- ❏ act for the greater good
- ❏ unravel the mystery of the Gulf War Syndrome
- ❏ travel to the source of the Nile at Lake Victoria
- ❏ build a pergola
- ❏ attend the Olympics
- ❏ take a llama pack trip through Montana's Crazy Mountains
- ❏ own a hot tub
- ❏ design decorative tiles
- ❏ attract cardinals to my bird feeder
- ❏ jog along the top of the Great Wall of China
- ❏ learn to make flatbread

- ❏ bottle the San Francisco fog
- ❏ see Cambodia's rice paddies in the spring
- ❏ dry my hydrangea blooms so I can enjoy them all year long
- ❏ ride an Icelandic pony across Iceland
- ❏ have a hybrid yellow-pink rose named after me
- ❏ refuse to be negative
- ❏ ....
- ❏ ....
- ❏ ....
- ❏ ....
- ❏ ....
- ❏ visit the ruins of Tikal, Guatemala
- ❏ experience a snowstorm in the Grand Canyon
- ❏ hire a welfare recipient
- ❏ put an end to toll roads
- ❏ learn to surf
- ❏ convert an old factory into living space
- ❏ visit Kitty Hawk, North Carolina

- ❏ join the pilgrimage around Kailas, the sacred mountain of Tibet
- ❏ treat my arthritis with diet and exercise
- ❏ hang glide off the Oregon coast
- ❏ ski the Tetons out of Jackson Hole, Wyoming
- ❏ hear Barbara Cook live
- ❏ learn how to manage my own stress
- ❏ build a campfire in the rain
- ❏ transform my autumn leaves into winter mulch
- ❏ learn to play golf
- ❏ visit Mexico's Parícutin Volcano
- ❏ make amends to those I've harmed
- ❏ see America before exploring abroad
- ❏ own a reverse dictionary that has the meaning first, then the word
- ❏ live beyond my means
- ❏ work for Amnesty International
- ❏ send a letter to the artist I most admire

- ❏ collect china dog figurines
- ❏ ride an all-terrain vehicle
- ❏ master the fine art of conversation
- ❏ find a use for my belly button
- ❏ toboggan in St. Moritz
- ❏ spend less time on the phone
- ❏ set a record at the golf range
- ❏ try, try again
- ❏ stay in bed all day with a box of bonbons and someone I love
- ❏ sandwich criticism between two layers of praise
- ❏ ....
- ❏ ....
- ❏ ....
- ❏ take a moral inventory of my life
- ❏ stop complaining
- ❏ not disappoint those who depend on me
- ❏ collect the sketches of a great theater designer
- ❏ campaign against strip malls
- ❏ save Mono Lake in California

- ❑ ride in a rodeo
- ❑ run a motel
- ❑ get married on the beach
- ❑ think critically, reason logically, speak articulately
- ❑ train clematis on a trellis
- ❑ know how to take and give hints
- ❑ memorize the preamble to the U.S. Constitution
- ❑ recognize and report one of the FBI's "most wanted"
- ❑ befriend a reference librarian
- ❑ temporarily walk away from my life
- ❑ follow directions
- ❑ praise my teammates
- ❑ get to work early
- ❑ walk underneath Victoria Falls, Zimbabwe
- ❑ ....
- ❑ ....
- ❑ ride the world's oldest roller coaster in Denmark's Tivoli Gardens
- ❑ keep a strong mental grip

- ❑ learn how to use my watch as a compass
- ❑ fly faster than Mach 1
- ❑ practice patriotism by actions, not rhetoric
- ❑ drink responsibly
- ❑ jog across the Coos Bay Bridge in Oregon
- ❑ look good in a bikini
- ❑ ....
- ❑ ....
- ❑ ....
- ❑ return every phone call on the day I receive it
- ❑ be in El Rosario, Mexico, when the monarch butterflies migrate
- ❑ shop till I drop
- ❑ drive defensively
- ❑ save money
- ❑ have see-through appliances so I can watch them work
- ❑ convince a policeman not to write the summons
- ❑ give the perfect rejoinder to an insult or snide remark—right then and there

- ❑ live in a palace
- ❑ explore the vineyards and pastures of the Shenandoah Valley
- ❑ ....
- ❑ clone myself and see my clone grow to maturity
- ❑ wear the green jacket of the Masters
- ❑ perfect virtual travel so I can see the world without leaving home
- ❑ be the only male in a harem of women or the only woman in a harem of men
- ❑ face a danger and overcome it
- ❑ see my children graduate from college debt-free
- ❑ perfect my recipe for Irish coffee
- ❑ collect exotic shells on the beaches of Sanibel and Captiva islands
- ❑ build and paint a wooden bird feeder
- ❑ invent creative uses for used satellite dishes
- ❑ learn welding

- ❏ raise my children to respect Earth
- ❏ furnish my house with antiques
- ❏ establish a weekly family-fun night
- ❏ give my spouse all I can give
- ❏ live near a foghorn
- ❏ learn the secrets of the great and apply them to my own life
- ❏ create a gourmet chef's kitchen
- ❏ find one uplifting message each day
- ❏ be someone's knight in shining armor
- ❏ sit in the front row at a play
- ❏ take the Cliff Walk in Newport, Rhode Island
- ❏ raise sunflowers
- ❏ write a fairy tale for my children about people and things they know

- ❏ find a meaningful career
- ❏ start a college fund for underprivileged students
- ❏ wear bright colors

- ❏ work for a growing company in a new, cutting-edge field
- ❏ volunteer to work with children with AIDS
- ❏ winter in Oaxaca, Mexico
- ❏ become an image consultant
- ❏ ....
- ❏ ....
- ❏ ....
- ❏ ....
- ❏ work two part-time jobs instead of one full-time job
- ❏ keep my memory sharp
- ❏ donate the vegetables from my garden to the local soup kitchen
- ❏ campaign against having an official language
- ❏ develop a multicultural perspective
- ❏ donate blood
- ❏ treat myself to a massage
- ❏ learn that my children believe I brought them up well
- ❏ act the age I feel, not the age I am

- ❏ hit the golf ball not just long but on the mark
- ❏ eliminate the negative tone from my conversation
- ❏ ....
- ❏ ....
- ❏ remember that life may be a puzzle, but the pieces fit
- ❏ have a tea blend created for and named after me
- ❏ travel to New Zealand's Chatham Islands
- ❏ knock on wood
- ❏ reserve a ticket on the space shuttle
- ❏ make a pitcher out of local clay
- ❏ see the Great Altar of Pergamum, in a museum in Berlin
- ❏ go tubing on a lazy, winding river
- ❏ plant morning glories on the fire escape
- ❏ keep a private stash of Mallomars
- ❏ get married in City Hall
- ❏ watch a caterpillar hatch into a butterfly and fly away

- ❏ file the keepsakes of my children
- ❏ start a fad that sweeps the nation
- ❏ forgo the frivolous and embrace what counts
- ❏ convert my house to solar energy
- ❏ help build a neighborhood senior center
- ❏ develop extrasensory perception
- ❏ record books for the blind
- ❏ stroll through the old section of Nice
- ❏ ....
- ❏ ....
- ❏ ....
- ❏ shop Seattle's Pike Place Market
- ❏ look good in hats
- ❏ go to opening day at the ballpark
- ❏ learn how to read palms
- ❏ campaign for the civil rights of legal immigrants
- ❏ eat an apple a day
- ❏ awake to steaming café au lait and flaky croissants in a Paris hotel
- ❏ have Barbra Streisand's fingernails

- ❑ tour the covered bridges of Bucks County, Pennsylvania
- ❑ make wind chimes
- ❑ confront prejudice whenever I hear it
- ❑ observe a spider spinning its web
- ❑ persuade my children that bicycle helmets are cool
- ❑ nourish creativity, starting with my own
- ❑ have a booth at a flea market
- ❑ get VIP treatment at a hotel
- ❑ teach what I most need to learn
- ❑ love my enemies
- ❑ ....
- ❑ ....
- ❑ ....
- ❑ ....
- ❑ see the land-diving in Vanuatu
- ❑ lessen my meals and lengthen my life
- ❑ see a blue iguana
- ❑ finish what I start
- ❑ build a fireplace in my house

- ❑ stop counting my chickens before they are hatched
- ❑ hear a glacier splitting
- ❑ avoid exaggeration of thought, word, or deed
- ❑ admit to my spouse that I was wrong, even in the heat of argument
- ❑ ....
- ❑ ....
- ❑ ride into the sunset with a gallant gaucho
- ❑ experience real virtue
- ❑ eschew fur
- ❑ volunteer at the local recreation department
- ❑ see a Cayman parrot
- ❑ be treated to my own individual video screen on an airplane
- ❑ sing all the choruses of "A Hundred Bottles of Beer on the Wall"—just once
- ❑ avoid extremes
- ❑ observe Christ's precepts, not just his birthday

- ❑ learn from the skilled
- ❑ practice tenderness
- ❑ remember all the words to "The Twelve Days of Christmas"
- ❑ own a lucky piece
- ❑ spend a summer Sunday in the hammock
- ❑ get married in the snow under a full moon
- ❑ keep at it after others have given up
- ❑ avoid contradicting people
- ❑ eat for pleasure
- ❑ take it easy on myself when I cannot make something happen
- ❑ shine my light on others
- ❑ reupholster the sofa
- ❑ trek to Ama Dablam, one of the Himalayan peaks in Nepal
- ❑ see electronic "cash" replace the use of currency
- ❑ have a javelina for a pet
- ❑ be the pause that refreshes
- ❑ ....
- ❑ ....

❑ see the battlefield at Gettysburg
❑ do the flower arrangements for a four-star
  restaurant
❑ plant a peach orchard
❑ eschew inertia
❑ eat a Howard Johnson's hot dog again
❑ shop in the Palo Alto shopping center—
  and wish that every mall could be this
  beautiful
❑ ....
❑ ....
❑ ....
❑ turn an old carriage house into a new
  residence
❑ be known as an innovator
❑ be part of a neighborhood watch group
❑ build a secret room in my house
❑ bank where the fees are lowest
❑ find the good in everyone
❑ take advantage of offerings of free
  entertainment
❑ be true to myself

- ❏ judge a book by its content, not by its cover
- ❏ keep quiet if I can't say anything nice
- ❏ spice my life with variety
- ❏ maintain a childlike innocence
- ❏ keep on learning new things
- ❏ ....
- ❏ ....
- ❏ ....
- ❏ talk to the locals wherever I go
- ❏ run a B&B on Maryland's eastern shore
- ❏ track a hurricane by plane
- ❏ be a torch singer
- ❏ own an original Volkswagen beetle—with a Maserati engine
- ❏ travel to Sikkim
- ❏ see the site of Washington's winter quarters at Valley Forge
- ❏ plant a weeping willow
- ❏ learn the technique of silk screening
- ❏ find outlets for my creativity
- ❏ have someone read *me* a bedtime story

- ❑ play night softball
- ❑ run a smoke-free vegetarian restaurant
- ❑ drive cross-country, playing and singing the scores of Broadway musicals
- ❑ have a mountain named for me
- ❑ stay on a ranch in Oklahoma
- ❑ serenade my beloved
- ❑ worship in a mosque
- ❑ hire someone to rake the leaves
- ❑ take flying lessons
- ❑ live more quietly
- ❑ learn to do less when it's not important
- ❑ learn to do more when it is important
- ❑ ....
- ❑ ....
- ❑ play hide-and-seek in a large house set in a large woods
- ❑ own an Etch A Sketch
- ❑ read in a tree
- ❑ make a crown of flowers
- ❑ send a fan letter anonymously

- ❏ spend a day at the Winding Stair Book Shop in Dublin
- ❏ own a 1952 Bugatti motorcycle
- ❏ write, produce, direct, and star in a movie
- ❏ build a stone bridge
- ❏ put a message on a billboard
- ❏ ....
- ❏ ....
- ❏ ....
- ❏ hold a Mayday celebration
- ❏ fingerpaint on butcher paper
- ❏ break old dishes to release my anger
- ❏ slide down the natural water chute on Kauai
- ❏ spend a romantic weekend with Val Kilmer
- ❏ give a magazine subscription as a gift
- ❏ dance in the moonlight
- ❏ "adopt" a person in a nursing home who has no relatives or visitors, and visit her regularly
- ❏ learn the varieties of paper
- ❏ build a dollhouse

- ❑ have my portrait taken by Richard Avedon
- ❑ own deerskin garden gloves
- ❑ be able to hear through walls
- ❑ help raise the percentage of people who vote
- ❑ accept myself, warts and all
- ❑ send out the laundry
- ❑ play
- ❑ share my feelings with my lover
- ❑ chalk a poem onto the sidewalk
- ❑ become a storyteller
- ❑ meditate as I walk
- ❑ realize that mistakes can be corrected
- ❑ ....
- ❑ ....
- ❑ identify what will fill the gaps in my life
- ❑ volunteer at the headquarters of the candidate of my choice
- ❑ do work that nourishes the soul
- ❑ slow my pace
- ❑ test my intelligence by challenging it

❑ force spring bulbs to blossom
❑ adhere to my car's maintenance schedule
❑ ....
❑ ....
❑ keep the spark of adventure alive
❑ overcome my fear of success
❑ wander around Sausalito and stop for a
   beer at the No Name Bar
❑ play Scarlett to Clark Gable's Rhett
❑ save the Great Barrier Reef
❑ have a mother like Maria in *The Sound
   of Music*
❑ identify everyone in old family
   photographs
❑ have an endless supply of truffles
❑ learn to e-mail a photo
❑ learn to download a photo
❑ eat an entire apple pie
❑ let my imagination soar
❑ read the morning
   newspaper in the morning
❑ be discerning

- ❏ learn to have fun on my own
- ❏ visit Queen Hatshepsut's temple in ancient Thebes
- ❏ be an extra in a Woody Allen movie
- ❏ climb Mount Olympus
- ❏ do a cartwheel
- ❏ expect my prayers to be answered
- ❏ ....
- ❏ ....
- ❏ ....
- ❏ keep a fire burning all day
- ❏ wear a shirtwaist dress again
- ❏ travel to Corsica
- ❏ have my home decorated by Alexandra Stoddard
- ❏ wear silk boxers
- ❏ have a favorite spot in the house that's mine alone
- ❏ become a theater makeup artist
- ❏ dress in white all year long
- ❏ consult a psychic
- ❏ be known for my exquisite taste

- ❑ become a personal fitness trainer
- ❑ ....
- ❑ ....
- ❑ ....
- ❑ serve as a mediator in an argument between two opposing parties
- ❑ repair old clocks
- ❑ participate in a videoconference
- ❑ persevere—even when I'm exhausted
- ❑ drive a motorcycle cross country
- ❑ own a monogrammed bathrobe
- ❑ train Seeing Eye dogs
- ❑ perform a service that makes a difference in my community
- ❑ pay my respects at Arlington National Cemetery
- ❑ drive a tank
- ❑ reach out to a deprived child
- ❑ learn to be an expert map reader
- ❑ free myself from fear
- ❑ pilot a streetcar
- ❑ know when to bite my tongue

- ❏ fight the defamation of homosexuals
- ❏ break a swimming record
- ❏ encourage the work of others
- ❏ run a toys-for-tots program
- ❏ complete a 25,000-piece puzzle
- ❏ teach my children a second language
- ❏ ski before work
- ❏ drive Virginia's Skyline Drive
- ❏ watch the Saturday morning 'toons with my children
- ❏ help extinguish forest fires
- ❏ feel empowered
- ❏ receive a fan letter
- ❏ become a motivational speaker
- ❏ ....
- ❏ ....
- ❏ ....
- ❏ ....
- ❏ cook a different ethnic meal every night for two weeks
- ❏ get a totally unexpected job offer
- ❏ live in a vacation destination

- ❏ alphabetize my library
- ❏ cross a swinging wooden suspension bridge over a gorge
- ❏ ....
- ❏ ....
- ❏ ....
- ❏ ....
- ❏ use the good china every day
- ❏ throw a "Let's Twist Again" party
- ❏ fall off a wall into the arms of friends
- ❏ build a bigger kitchen
- ❏ travel on a shoestring budget
- ❏ spend a day touring the train stations of Paris
- ❏ build a yellow brick road to my doorstep
- ❏ learn the art of relaxation
- ❏ notice daily miracles
- ❏ celebrate daily miracles
- ❏ crumple up my to-do list
- ❏ trust my own way of doing things
- ❏ invite my parents somewhere they've never been

- ❑ walk aimlessly
- ❑ pet a snake
- ❑ swim in a quarry
- ❑ donate my car to charity
- ❑ open my home to someone in need
- ❑ investigate my dark side
- ❑ live in a yurt
- ❑ ride a "century"—i.e., bike 100 miles in a single day
- ❑ do an ink drawing of my lover
- ❑ live with my parents again—briefly
- ❑ live with my children again—briefly
- ❑ ....
- ❑ ....
- ❑ invent a new language
- ❑ buy a toboggan
- ❑ repair the hole in the ozone
- ❑ question authority
- ❑ walk along a railroad track
- ❑ spend a day with my ears blocked to experience deafness
- ❑ orbit the Earth

- ❑ put on a slicker and go out in the rain
- ❑ spend a day atop the Eiffel Tower to photograph Paris in the changing light
- ❑ become my own catalyst for change
- ❑ study music in Rome
- ❑ become a translator
- ❑ be the first person to fly in Leonardo da Vinci's wings
- ❑ ....
- ❑ ....
- ❑ ....
- ❑ ....
- ❑ make one perfect flower arrangement
- ❑ appreciate the value of time
- ❑ learn to focus like a laser
- ❑ pack my backpack and go
- ❑ stage a Beatles marathon
- ❑ play a pickup game of basketball in a Detroit playground
- ❑ see a tornado close up—but not *too* close
- ❑ change what isn't working
- ❑ build a bamboo fence

- ❏ endow a library
- ❏ surf along the sand dunes of the Lake Michigan shoreline
- ❏ change the political system
- ❏ find the mystical in the mundane
- ❏ own a piece of Ebbetts Field
- ❏ work the apple harvest in Washington state

- ❏ pub-crawl in Dublin
- ❏ go to a movie all by myself on a weekday afternoon
- ❏ get a house for free
- ❏ make my living as an artist
- ❏ travel in the realm of the spirit
- ❏ become a wrangler
- ❏ bump into an old friend at the train station in Budapest
- ❏ join a barter exchange
- ❏ forgive my past mistakes and move on
- ❏ follow my heart's yearnings
- ❏ stop forgetting my locker combination
- ❏ become a book reviewer on the Internet

❑ throw a lavish dinner with place cards
❑ act as if it were my duty to be happy
❑ study Sanskrit
❑ experience complete anonymity
❑ find the perfect someone with whom to
  share my life
❑ see a President of the United States invite
  the *losing* team to the White House
❑ scuba dive off Malta
❑ work at my own pace
❑ do what I need to do to have what I
  want to have
❑ be named Teacher of the Year
❑ live near a Super Kmart
❑ ....
❑ ....
❑ go back in time and meet Laura Ingalls
  Wilder
❑ see my ship come in
❑ drive to South America on the Pan-
  American Highway
❑ maintain courtesy at all times

- ❑ discover a great junk store
- ❑ make a habit of using cologne
- ❑ redecorate my home in blue and white
- ❑ ....
- ❑ ....
- ❑ ....
- ❑ design a dress
- ❑ watch my babies being born
- ❑ publish a newsletter
- ❑ run into my best friend from elementary school
- ❑ own a Rolex watch
- ❑ retrace the journeys of the indomitable Isabella Bird
- ❑ learn what I can live without
- ❑ have tea at the Shelburne in Dublin
- ❑ expect the best
- ❑ open a store
- ❑ go back to school
- ❑ be in the audience for *A Prairie Home Companion*
- ❑ become a naturalist

- ❑ put a five-dollar bill in one pocket of all my winter clothes before storing them for the summer
- ❑ learn to play the clarinet
- ❑ avoid the news for a week
- ❑ see Devil's Slide, the cliff-bound California coast, south of San Francisco
- ❑ excavate and restore buried dreams
- ❑ work the night shift
- ❑ be awarded a grant to go to art school
- ❑ identify and document a previously unknown species of plant or animal
- ❑ raise quarter horses
- ❑ win a Ford Explorer in a contest
- ❑ sign a book contract
- ❑ learn to do needlepoint
- ❑ write a letter to myself each day
- ❑ bake gingerbread
- ❑ ....
- ❑ ....
- ❑ ....
- ❑ walk through my childhood home again

- ❑ line my eyes with kohl
- ❑ know how to choose the right moment to open my mouth
- ❑ be in perfect sync with my boss
- ❑ seize every opportunity
- ❑ satisfy my wanderlust
- ❑ see my grandparents' house again
- ❑ rekindle hope
- ❑ ....
- ❑ ....
- ❑ ....
- ❑ exercise for an hour before breakfast
- ❑ run a transport service for kids going to sports practice
- ❑ sleep with the door open
- ❑ possess a unique point of view
- ❑ become a master electrician
- ❑ discover my adolescent belongings in a box in the attic
- ❑ treat myself with generosity
- ❑ see my name in lights
- ❑ clean only my own room

- ❏ write a new chapter of my life—and give it a happy ending
- ❏ eat alphabet soup and crackers in bed
- ❏ be awakened by a kiss from Prince Charming
- ❏ ....
- ❏ ....
- ❏ ....
- ❏ ....
- ❏ bake a perfect *tarte tatin*
- ❏ take time each day for a pleasant memory
- ❏ own an English club chair with a tufted ottoman
- ❏ contribute to research on macular degeneration
- ❏ dive the soft coral forests of Bequia
- ❏ hand-pump water from a well
- ❏ sleep for twelve hours
- ❏ start a hope chest
- ❏ take a weekend retreat in a convent
- ❏ savor life's small moments
- ❏ own a wicker picnic hamper

- ❑ wire a dollhouse for real electric lighting
- ❑ venture into the wilderness
- ❑ look as good as my mother does when I'm her age
- ❑ set the sail, weigh anchor, and feel the wind at my back
- ❑ learn to play the harp
- ❑ dye my own wool
- ❑ speak a foreign language without having to study it
- ❑ get an answer from the Delphic Oracle
- ❑ dine by candlelight, even when alone
- ❑ wear bright red lipstick
- ❑ hang strings of garlic and chilies in the kitchen
- ❑ be ready for the unforeseen
- ❑ hear an angel whispering in my ear
- ❑ be a first-rate version of myself, not a second-rate imitation of someone else
- ❑ get a promotion
- ❑ possess true grit and amazing grace

- ❏ build my own skylit studio in the woods
- ❏ put an end to child pornography
- ❏ learn to dance the two-step
- ❏ travel to Bhutan
- ❏ make madeleines
- ❏ go on a shopping spree at The Body Shop
- ❏ see the Valley of the Kings in Egypt
- ❏ make a shelter out of mosquito netting for bug-free summer dining outdoors
- ❏ visit the Grand Tetons
- ❏ stop taking myself so seriously
- ❏ visit Half Moon Bay on the California coast
- ❏ ....
- ❏ ....
- ❏ ....
- ❏ ....
- ❏ be invited to the Iowa Writers' Workshop
- ❏ go a whole day without becoming angry
- ❏ work overseas
- ❏ watch a movie in a theater with no crying babies or talking

- ❏ be able to identify cloud formations
- ❏ manage a roadside vegetable stand
- ❏ visit Yellowstone National Park in the dead of winter
- ❏ begin a Barbie doll collection
- ❏ take time each afternoon for a cup of tea and reflection on the day's events
- ❏ keel a catamaran
- ❏ go winter camping on snowshoes
- ❏ start a business with my spouse
- ❏ scuba dive the Ngemelis Drop-Off of Palau's barrier reef
- ❏ acquire a taste for malt whisky
- ❏ be moved by a spiritual leader
- ❏ teach college
- ❏ watch cheese being made in Wisconsin
- ❏ feel that I've made it in life
- ❏ switch to an ergonomic keyboard
- ❏ spend a weekend watching classic movies
- ❏ watch a speed race at Bonneville Salt Flats in Utah
- ❏ do work I'm proud to put my name to

- ❑ wash my hair in rainwater
- ❑ operate a market stall in an exotic bazaar
- ❑ make a sand painting out of the colored sands of the Mojave
- ❑ paint my living room bright red
- ❑ win fame
- ❑ tell all on a talk show
- ❑ make my whole family nutrition-conscious
- ❑ own a cartouche with my name written in hieroglyphics
- ❑ carry a Grace Kelly handbag by Hermès
- ❑ achieve a perfect lotus pose in yoga
- ❑ ....
- ❑ ....
- ❑ possess panache
- ❑ see what life is like as a cloistered nun
- ❑ wear red leather cowboy boots
- ❑ hunt tigers
- ❑ entertain like Martha Stewart
- ❑ learn tai chi—and do it for the rest of my life
- ❑ buy vintage linens

❑ embark on a road trip this weekend
❑ ....
❑ ....
❑ ....
❑ ....
❑ take my pet to a holistic veterinarian
❑ cover London theater for the local paper
❑ heal a breach
❑ be a favorite of children
❑ lower my voice
❑ compose a song for Mary Chapin
   Carpenter
❑ in Ireland, eat smoked salmon and capers
   on soda bread and wash it down with
   single-malt Bushmills
❑ fly through the air with the greatest
   of ease
❑ shop in consignment stores
❑ see a man get pregnant
❑ wear a Donna Karan original
❑ fill my house with Jean Michel Frank
   furniture

- ❑ be photographed in the nude—and like the results
- ❑ dabble in mysticism
- ❑ ....
- ❑ ....
- ❑ bicycle through Holland when the tulips are in bloom
- ❑ bake popovers
- ❑ time-travel to the 17th century and come to the New World with its first European settlers
- ❑ read Sigrid Unset's trilogy, *Kristin Lavransdatter*
- ❑ be a panelist on *Meet the Press*
- ❑ see the *Moses* by Michelangelo in Rome
- ❑ call for order in the Supreme Court
- ❑ fight boredom
- ❑ read all of Agatha Christie's books
- ❑ have a typical French *pique-nique sur l'herbes:* bread, cheese, sausage, and wine
- ❑ set up a large trust fund for my daughter

- ❏ memorize the periodic table of the elements—again
- ❏ see my child win a championship
- ❏ make love on the beach without getting sandy
- ❏ ....
- ❏ ....
- ❏ scuba dive the Bikini atoll
- ❏ twirl a baton
- ❏ invent a new "disaster" for a Hollywood disaster movie
- ❏ spoil my grandchildren
- ❏ go on a flea-market tour of America
- ❏ read ancient ruins the way a detective reads clues
- ❏ direct a television show
- ❏ eliminate clutter
- ❏ find the mystical in the mundane
- ❏ really start fresh on New Year's Day
- ❏ have a million dollars in the bank
- ❏ collect 18th-century furniture
- ❏ interview the mayor for the local paper

- ❑ see the "Little Mermaid" statue in Copenhagen
- ❑ wear a felt fedora
- ❑ own a voice-activated VCR
- ❑ use Chanel No. 5 soap, lotion, talc, and perfume
- ❑ replace all my dish towels
- ❑ produce a record
- ❑ possess a deep voice
- ❑ unearth an ancient wall painting on an archaeological dig
- ❑ go back and make different choices in life
- ❑ light candles throughout the house on Candlemas
- ❑ slow down
- ❑ collect old issues of *Seventeen* magazine
- ❑ own a Steiff teddy bear
- ❑ visit Monet's house at Giverny
- ❑ tour the Waterford factory and buy a sample glass
- ❑ surround myself with things I love

- ❑ drive a tow truck
- ❑ take the waters at the original Spa, in Belgium
- ❑ ....
- ❑ ....
- ❑ ....
- ❑ ....
- ❑ receive unconditional love
- ❑ light a candle in church every week
- ❑ wear Katharine Hepburn trousers
- ❑ learn how to open my heart to others
- ❑ take one step forward and no steps back
- ❑ volunteer in a political campaign
- ❑ bewitch a man
- ❑ see my house used as the set in a movie
- ❑ be able to laugh at myself
- ❑ start drinking decaffeinated coffee
- ❑ trust my instincts
- ❑ give a business suit to a homeless person who is looking for a job
- ❑ write my will
- ❑ have dinner with my Senator

- ❏ become a Wall Street broker
- ❏ host a week-long game of Diplomacy
- ❏ ....
- ❏ ....
- ❏ go to camp
- ❏ buy Ralph Lauren sheets and blankets
- ❏ feel comfortable asking others for favors
- ❏ put on a burlap sack, belt it, and call it a dress
- ❏ get a mud-pack facial
- ❏ go behind the scenes at *Hard Copy*
- ❏ argue a case before the Supreme Court
- ❏ make gooseberry jam
- ❏ have teeth like people on toothpaste commercials
- ❏ know what I am not
- ❏ close a million-dollar movie deal
- ❏ rearrange the furniture
- ❏ attend the Miss America pageant
- ❏ rent a beach house in the Hamptons on Long Island
- ❏ collect antique children's books

- ❏ anchor the nightly news
- ❏ organize my personal papers
- ❏ see to it that my home is a safe haven
- ❏ howl at the moon
- ❏ worship among the spires, pinnacles, and arches of Canyonlands National Park
- ❏ make a video of my typical day
- ❏ dine on caviar while seated on orange crates
- ❏ approach the day's tasks with reverence
- ❏ sign an endorsement deal
- ❏ rearrange all the pictures on the wall
- ❏ ....
- ❏ ....
- ❏ get a manicure
- ❏ make cowslip wine
- ❏ organize the Tupperware by size and shape
- ❏ browse the secondhand bookstands along the banks of the Seine in Paris
- ❏ unexpectedly inherit a fortune
- ❏ toss out last year's accumulated guilt

- ❑ celebrate Christmas on shipboard
- ❑ build a window seat for rainy-day escapes
- ❑ eschew deprivation
- ❑ act out my fantasies
- ❑ see the Jakobshavn Glacier in Greenland, the world's fastest-moving glacier
- ❑ clean out my drawers
- ❑ get elected to national office
- ❑ have someone write a song for me
- ❑ attend Carneval in Rio de Janeiro
- ❑ polish the silver
- ❑ see how the other half lives
- ❑ nurse a baby
- ❑ cross a wild continent
- ❑ be stopped at a toad crossing on a British road
- ❑ ....
- ❑ ....
- ❑ ....
- ❑ eat fats, cholesterol, nitrites, salt, food dyes, and preservatives with abandon
- ❑ feel welcome wherever I go

- ❑ try a luxurious new bath product every day for a month
- ❑ pay attention to the details
- ❑ manage a research and development operation in a major technology company
- ❑ ....
- ❑ ....
- ❑ ....
- ❑ revel in my desires
- ❑ explore the byways of London's Camden Town
- ❑ have children who do not need orthodontia
- ❑ attend a play by the Theater of the Deaf
- ❑ travel to Uruguay
- ❑ take a flying lesson from John Travolta
- ❑ sacrifice appearance to quality
- ❑ collect Delft pottery
- ❑ plant a rose garden
- ❑ visit the Friesian Islands, off the Netherlands, whose people were the first to support American independence
- ❑ roll up the rugs and dance

- ❑ know when enough is enough
- ❑ display my most cherished possession
- ❑ try something new
- ❑ give myself a Mother's Day gift
- ❑ forgive myself for failing to live up to my own expectations
- ❑ remember to change the baking soda in the refrigerator
- ❑ ....
- ❑ ....
- ❑ ....
- ❑ fall in love at first sight
- ❑ ride a horse through Wales
- ❑ prepare my children to act as adults
- ❑ cure a ham
- ❑ get rid of what is no longer useful
- ❑ get rid of what no longer seems beautiful
- ❑ have dinner with Roseanne
- ❑ hire someone to wash all the windows
- ❑ toot my own horn
- ❑ accumulate a new wardrobe slowly
- ❑ throw a theme costume party

- ❏ know where everything is
- ❏ make one frivolous purchase each month
- ❏ build a flagstone patio
- ❏ ....
- ❏ ....
- ❏ travel to the Sudan
- ❏ design a tablecloth
- ❏ take the ferry from Europe to Asia across the straits of the Bosporous
- ❏ possess a debit card
- ❏ go out on a date with my spouse on Saturday night
- ❏ become a roustabout in the North Sea oil fields
- ❏ swim in all five Great Lakes
- ❏ ice-skate backwards
- ❏ attend the Lincoln Center Festival in New York in the summer
- ❏ go disco dancing
- ❏ become an architect of public spaces
- ❏ in a university archive, study the actual papers of William Faulkner

- ❑ see the pink palaces of Jaipur, India
- ❑ collect antique buttons
- ❑ catch the Hail Mary pass in the end zone, with only seconds to go
- ❑ be paired with Pete Sampras in tennis doubles
- ❑ play hooky from work
- ❑ keep my resolutions
- ❑ live briefly in a society that does not permit freedom of expression
- ❑ ....
- ❑ ....
- ❑ attend a Spice Girls concert
- ❑ let off steam
- ❑ find a buyer for my house in two weeks
- ❑ know the nicknames of all the states
- ❑ kayak the Gauley River of West Virginia
- ❑ own a really good reading lamp
- ❑ have an expert check my home's *feng shui*
- ❑ learn to ride a cutting horse
- ❑ grow up with both mother and father in the same house

- ❏ ....
- ❏ ....
- ❏ ....
- ❏ ....
- ❏ experience fame
- ❏ translate the erotic poems of Catullus into English verse
- ❏ become a sensation on the London stage
- ❏ drive safely through a blizzard
- ❏ have a comma in my bank balance
- ❏ go to the top of Toronto's CN Tower, the world's tallest building
- ❏ carry a love charm
- ❏ go to a game of the Women's NBA
- ❏ refresh myself in summer with a dab of lavender water
- ❏ apply for a fellowship
- ❏ retreat for a week to a Buddhist monastery
- ❏ indulge my wants
- ❏ earn more money than my parents did, less than my children will
- ❏ have webbed hands so I can swim faster

- ❑ manage to be at the right place at the right time
- ❑ line all my clothes drawers with scented paper
- ❑ burn dried thyme in the fireplace
- ❑ let flowers overflow in the window box
- ❑ ....
- ❑ ....
- ❑ ....
- ❑ feel the exultation felt by the pre-midnight Cinderella
- ❑ sleep in a canopied four-poster bed
- ❑ transform tattered curtains into a quaint-looking wall hanging
- ❑ desktop-publish my own business cards
- ❑ wear a beret
- ❑ plant daffodils and tulips as perennial harbingers of spring
- ❑ remember the combination to my gym locker, bike, and suitcase locks
- ❑ double-dig a flower bed
- ❑ reinvent myself

- ❏ become a transatlantic celebrity
- ❏ find a quiet refuge outdoors where I can gather my thoughts
- ❏ learn to whistle
- ❏ choose not to focus on what may be missing in my life
- ❏ visit John O'Groats, at the top of Scotland
- ❏ taste blackberry cordial
- ❏ learn fencing
- ❏ ....
- ❏ ....
- ❏ turn my refrigerator door into an art gallery of my children's works
- ❏ ask forgiveness of all the people I have hurt
- ❏ become an overnight success
- ❏ excel at project management
- ❏ see the crown jewels in the Tower of London
- ❏ go to a shipboard party
- ❏ hike the Long Trail of Vermont from Massachusetts to Canada

- ❑ ....
- ❑ ....
- ❑ live frugally
- ❑ create a completely self-sufficient lifestyle
- ❑ be able to disregard the price tag when I see something I want
- ❑ experiment with life
- ❑ play Horatio in a full-scale production of *Hamlet*
- ❑ remember everything I read
- ❑ have a romance with an Italian man who speaks no English
- ❑ trek from the Jordan River to the Mediterranean Sea
- ❑ eat the oysters of France's Arcachon Bay
- ❑ create my own luck
- ❑ find a use for everything
- ❑ plant the seeds of possibility
- ❑ enjoy a comfortable cushion of savings
- ❑ keep my sense of humor no matter what happens
- ❑ become an arbitrager

- ❏ shed ambition
- ❏ study the teachings of Buddha
- ❏ swallow the watermelon seeds
- ❏ float in a balsa raft westward from Peru
- ❏ find out whether or not O. J. did it
- ❏ campaign against cellular phones in cars
- ❏ learn to love weeding
- ❏ cook double portions of my favorite recipes and freeze half
- ❏ get a standing ovation
- ❏ start a standing ovation
- ❏ fry chicken like the Colonel
- ❏ own less
- ❏ rake my neighbor's yard
- ❏ refuse to feel humiliation
- ❏ ....
- ❏ ....
- ❏ ....
- ❏ try tofu
- ❏ be able to play Scott Joplin rags on the piano

- ❏ eat popcorn in bed

- ❑ scuba dive the Blue Hole off Belize
- ❑ crush grapes
- ❑ ....
- ❑ ....
- ❑ ....
- ❑ spend a week on a beach with a suitcase full of books
- ❑ sculpt the face of a mountain
- ❑ spend a day alone in a petting zoo—just me and the animals
- ❑ campaign against the littering of outer space
- ❑ have dinner with Barbra Streisand
- ❑ go back in time and meet my parents when they met each other
- ❑ bake the perfect blueberry pie
- ❑ shuck the business suit for leotards and an oversized shirt
- ❑ ride a wide-gauge train
- ❑ get a pound of Beluga caviar as a gift
- ❑ learn to like roller coasters
- ❑ own a solid-gold swizzle stick

- ❑ attend the inauguration of the first woman President
- ❑ operate a gift basket business
- ❑ find a hidden talent
- ❑ climb Ayers Rock in Australia
- ❑ make a great speech
- ❑ taste Neapolitan chocolate
- ❑ invent the pit-free cherry
- ❑ keep a bookie, accountant, and lawyer on retainer
- ❑ ....
- ❑ ....
- ❑ ....
- ❑ shop at a private sample sale
- ❑ create a raised-bed garden
- ❑ live by my wits
- ❑ learn to yodel
- ❑ luxuriate on a houseboat in Kashmir
- ❑ stay at the Palumbo in Ravello on Italy's Amalfi Coast and breakfast overlooking the azure Mediterranean
- ❑ juggle flaming torches

- ❑ attend greyhound races
- ❑ build a greenhouse and have living things year-round
- ❑ find gold and stake my claim
- ❑ be godparent to a friend's child
- ❑ attend a playwriting workshop
- ❑ live on New York City's Park Avenue
- ❑ organize and replace items in the spice rack
- ❑ ....
- ❑ ....
- ❑ attend the Frankfurt Book Fair
- ❑ search for the Abominable Snowman in the Himalayas
- ❑ prepare for the unexpected
- ❑ be unintimidated by the fact that I make less money than my mate
- ❑ call in "well"
- ❑ cross a frozen river on a sleigh
- ❑ spend a night in the historic Shepheard's Hotel in Cairo
- ❑ enjoy Las Vegas on an expense account

❑ ....
❑ ....
❑ ....
❑ ....
❑ see wild guanacos in the Andes
❑ strike up a conversation with a stranger
❑ record an oral history of the family
❑ win at blackjack
❑ go for a midnight skinny-dip with someone,
   then dry off together
❑ build a grape arbor
❑ drink from blue-tinted crystal
❑ subscribe to *The National Enquirer*
❑ enter a backgammon tournament
❑ solve the conflict between family and
   career
❑ buy a one-way bus ticket to wherever $100
   will take me and just start fresh
❑ mull cider
❑ see the "Big Room" in Carlsbad Caverns
❑ pack my own pillow when I travel
❑ reveal a secret crush

- ❑ choreograph a pas de deux for my lover and me
- ❑ sail-ski across Greenland's ice cap
- ❑ clean off my desk
- ❑ invest in a small start-up company that becomes a huge success
- ❑ make bagels
- ❑ paint a mural on my wall
- ❑ win a fishing derby
- ❑ discover an archaeological site in my hometown
- ❑ make eggnog
- ❑ spend a luxurious weekend at the Ritz-Carlton in Boston
- ❑ learn to navigate by the stars
- ❑ ....
- ❑ ....
- ❑ ....
- ❑ deck the halls with boughs of holly
- ❑ act one of the great Shakespearean roles
- ❑ wake up cheerful
- ❑ tour the bridges of Madison County

- ❑ spend a warm spring **day** at the races
- ❑ play the devil's advocate
- ❑ overcome an old fear
- ❑ camp in my truck
- ❑ see a performance of the Spanish Riding Academy
- ❑ be able to change a bicycle tire in 5 minutes, a car tire in 15
- ❑ eat a Parker House roll at the Parker House in Boston
- ❑ ....
- ❑ ....
- ❑ become a paleontologist
- ❑ attend fly-fishing school
- ❑ observe M42, the Orion nebula
- ❑ walk the Street of the Dead in Teotihuacán
- ❑ invent a personal prayer of thanks for Thanksgiving
- ❑ practice organic gardening
- ❑ make it to the finals of the National Geography Bee
- ❑ live and travel in a French gypsy cart

- ❏ invent underwear that doesn't wedgie
- ❏ visit the places where Buddha lived
- ❏ make copies of old family photographs
- ❏ scuba dive in the Galapagos
- ❏ let a ringing phone go unanswered
- ❏ wear a low-cut black satin dress
- ❏ travel to the Bay of Plenty, New Zealand— just for the name
- ❏ live to see them find a cure for spinal-cord injuries
- ❏ have a personal astrologer
- ❏ understand Nietzsche
- ❏ shoot billiards in the pool hall
- ❏ produce a television show that becomes the all-time most-watched program
- ❏ have a house with perfect plumbing
- ❏ call the Psychic Friends Network
- ❏ be able to quote from *Les Fleurs du Mal* of Baudelaire
- ❏ ....
- ❏ ....
- ❏ ....

- ❑ exercise muscles I never even knew I had
- ❑ wear fabulous earrings
- ❑ go on a second honeymoon
- ❑ ....
- ❑ ....
- ❑ become the disk jockey of a radio show
  that plays only women vocalists,
  musicians, composers
- ❑ go back in time and visit what was once
  the U.S.S.R.
- ❑ develop all five senses
- ❑ have a power lunch at the fabled Four
  Seasons restaurant in New York
- ❑ collect old *American Heritage* magazines
- ❑ master calculators
- ❑ see a performance of *Amahl and the Night
  Visitors* every Christmas
- ❑ become the new Billy Wilder
- ❑ learn to say "I love you" in ten different
  languages
- ❑ scuba dive under the ice pack of Antarctica
- ❑ read Dante's *Divine Comedy*

- ❑ volunteer in a beach cleanup
- ❑ see Bridalveil Falls in Yosemite National Park
- ❑ travel to the site of the ancient Ur of the Chaldees in Iraq
- ❑ dress in a jumpsuit
- ❑ hike the Alps wearing lederhosen and carrying an alpenstock
- ❑ discover a previously unknown subatomic particle
- ❑ buy recycled paper only
- ❑ ....
- ❑ ....
- ❑ ....
- ❑ make a perfect *pesto* sauce
- ❑ ride in the back of a stretch limo
- ❑ see the temples of Abu Simbel in Egypt
- ❑ own a tractor mower
- ❑ invent a male birth control pill
- ❑ become a volunteer reading tutor
- ❑ out of the blue, telephone the person with whom I went to the senior prom

❑ produce my own multimedia shows on my
    computer monitor

❑ ....

❑ ....

❑ ....

❑ write a great love story

❑ attend butler school

❑ climb Cotopaxi in Ecuador, the world's
    highest active volcano

❑ change the furniture to fit the season

❑ sail throughout Indonesia

❑ eat when hungry, sleep when tired

❑ receive a MacArthur "genius" grant

❑ own a radio station

❑ dress in plastic clothing

❑ have a studio on the Ile de la Cité in Paris

❑ attend a couples' massage workshop

❑ explore Mammoth Cave National Park by
    boat

❑ find a reminder system that works

❑ realize a dream deferred

❑ resolve never to go to bed angry

- ❑ tile my entire bathroom—floor, walls, ceiling—with ceramic tiles from Italy
- ❑ own a Mason-Pearson hairbrush
- ❑ ....
- ❑ ....
- ❑ ....
- ❑ wear a leather suit
- ❑ be mistaken for Cindy Crawford
- ❑ become a florist
- ❑ have dinner with Whoopi Goldberg
- ❑ get a magnum of champagne and five friends and have a party
- ❑ see the pre-Columbian Indian mounds of Shiloh National Park
- ❑ learn to play handball
- ❑ take a beer-lover's tour of Belgium
- ❑ give a great toast at a friend's wedding
- ❑ go whitewater rafting on the Green River in Colorado
- ❑ win at Twister
- ❑ learn to play the recorder

- ❑ create an Advent calendar
- ❑ ....
- ❑ ....
- ❑ see a ballet by Jerome Robbins
- ❑ perfect my tennis serve
- ❑ pop colored popcorn
- ❑ understand semiotics
- ❑ eat food without condiments to appreciate the genuine taste and texture
- ❑ collect dolls from many countries
- ❑ explore Utah's Escalante Wilderness
- ❑ build up my biceps
- ❑ have dinner with Bill Gates
- ❑ take a gourmet picnic from Spago to a Hollywood Bowl concert
- ❑ read all the *Little House* books of Laura Ingalls Wilder to my child, just as my mother read them to me
- ❑ plant a shade garden
- ❑ make a salad of yucca flower petals
- ❑ own a great atlas—on CD-ROM
- ❑ become a test driver

- ❑ have dinner with Bryant Gumbel
- ❑ grab the brass ring
- ❑ live in a Colonial-era farmhouse with a stone fireplace in the kitchen
- ❑ allow no phone calls during dinner: it's family time
- ❑ be able to dress for work in sweats
- ❑ show gratitude
- ❑ discover an extraterrestrial life-form in my garage
- ❑ keep my house spotless
- ❑ own a minicassette recorder so I can hold on to those brilliant ideas that pop into my mind and pop right back out
- ❑ stop overscheduling
- ❑ ....
- ❑ ....
- ❑ be in bed by 10:00 P.M.
- ❑ shop for books on the Internet
- ❑ find a sport I enjoy
- ❑ find a sport I'm good at
- ❑ learn to be at ease speaking in public

- [ ] carry a one-hundred-dollar bill in a secret compartment for emergencies
- [ ] attend a mystery weekend and solve the mystery
- [ ] ....
- [ ] ....
- [ ] ....
- [ ] have drinks by the pool of the Royal Palm Hotel on Grand Bay, Mauritius
- [ ] descend the grand staircase of the Paris Opera House in formal dress as flashbulbs pop
- [ ] live in the moment
- [ ] have someone ask if I've lost weight
- [ ] go on vacation and leave my watch at home
- [ ] have a numbered Swiss bank account
- [ ] ride the Pony Express National Historic Trail on horseback
- [ ] practice goodness
- [ ] have my children get up, get dressed, and get out the door without my fussing at them

- ❑ feast on *pissaladière* in Nice
- ❑ memorize the opening of the Declaration of Independence
- ❑ ....
- ❑ ....
- ❑ ....
- ❑ ....
- ❑ attend an Ivy League college
- ❑ be able to read the clouds and predict the weather
- ❑ become a movie reviewer
- ❑ have a swimming pool in my apartment building
- ❑ organize a community Easter egg hunt
- ❑ own a powerful juice-making machine
- ❑ get my name in the tabloids
- ❑ learn to play lacrosse
- ❑ see the pink rattlesnakes in the Grand Canyon
- ❑ sing in cabarets
- ❑ become a book illustrator
- ❑ search for *Homo erectus* in Java

- ❑ learn how to tie a bow tie
- ❑ imagine one good short story
- ❑ make love on a yacht
- ❑ look good sleeping
- ❑ see the Chicago Cubs win the World Series
- ❑ install a talking dictionary on my computer
- ❑ plan and run a weeklong conference at an exotic location
- ❑ travel to Minorca
- ❑ furnish my house entirely with wicker furniture
- ❑ visit all the lighthouses on the Atlantic and Pacific coasts
- ❑ teach English in Prague for a year
- ❑ wear a panama hat
- ❑ go kayaking among a pod of humpback whales
- ❑ fish from a float boat
- ❑ drop out and travel for a year
- ❑ ....
- ❑ ....
- ❑ see Times Square at night

- ❑ enjoy the pursuit of tickets to a supposedly sold-out show
- ❑ take lessons in Latin dancing
- ❑ ....
- ❑ ....
- ❑ become a great punster
- ❑ mend a fishing net
- ❑ finally throw out pens that don't work
- ❑ hear Big Ben chime
- ❑ become a professional jockey
- ❑ make a perfect three-minute egg
- ❑ never say "never"
- ❑ devise a way to keep the pots-and-pans cupboard organized
- ❑ pick off a would-be base stealer
- ❑ be part of a potluck Thanksgiving celebration with "chosen family"
- ❑ live in the Bohemian neighborhood of a large city
- ❑ do a 360 on my skateboard
- ❑ own *Webster's Third,* the version scholars say is best

❑ build a toothpick model of the Eiffel Tower
❑ play the harmonica or washboard
❑ photograph town landmarks and
   turn them into postcards
❑ become a puppeteer
❑ play water polo
❑ see the hospital where I was born
❑ remember to praise my children often
❑ do a backspin serve in table tennis
❑ become a Hollywood stuntman
❑ ....
❑ ....
❑ ....
❑ master the bank deposit and the neck-and-
   neck—trick pool shots
❑ create my own wrapping paper
❑ make a Christmas tree ornament
❑ put a sundial in the backyard
❑ be considered a strong leader
❑ explore Muir Woods
❑ write down all the weird things I've always
   wondered about

- ❑ do my best in whatever I'm doing
- ❑ eat authentic hush puppies in Alabama
- ❑ pour concrete
- ❑ build a snow family
- ❑ slip a love note into the book my mate is reading
- ❑ wear shoes that don't match
- ❑ get four empty seats across on my next long flight, so I can stretch out and sleep
- ❑ understand Euclidean geometry
- ❑ visit the Tupperware Museum
- ❑ take the family on an adventure vacation
- ❑ star in *Cyrano de Bergerac*
- ❑ ....
- ❑ ....
- ❑ ....
- ❑ see the catacombs of Alexandria
- ❑ study psychology
- ❑ keep a record of the good things that happen
- ❑ see the dinosaur footprints in the Grand Canyon

- ❑ become a state legislator
- ❑ carry a sketchbook
- ❑ open an eco-tourism resort in Central America
- ❑ ....
- ❑ ....
- ❑ ....
- ❑ streak my hair blond
- ❑ eat at a truck stop off the Interstate at four in the morning
- ❑ move to a bigger house
- ❑ move to a smaller house
- ❑ take ballet lessons
- ❑ prune my own trees
- ❑ make a hole-in-one in front of witnesses
- ❑ take a class in life drawing
- ❑ stop working on weekends
- ❑ be carried across the threshold
- ❑ spend the summer in a thatched cottage on the Dingle Peninsula
- ❑ donate books I no longer read to a psychiatric ward

❑ assist on a photo shoot for *Life* magazine
❑ make homemade potato chips
❑ serve on a grand jury
❑ learn to repot plants
❑ learn to play the drums
❑ be considered a "cool"
   parent by my children's friends
❑ ....
❑ ....
❑ be stranded on a Pacific island with my
   mate, where the only distraction is
   each other
❑ be mentioned in *People* magazine
❑ promise myself something nice . . .
❑ . . . deliver on my promise
❑ balloon across Switzerland
❑ spend one weekend a month on the road
❑ venture off the beaten path
❑ like Huck Finn, light out for the territory
❑ stay in the Chateau Frontenac in Quebec
❑ wash my lover's hair
❑ understand the other person's point of view

- ❑ be a party planner
- ❑ ....
- ❑ ....
- ❑ ....
- ❑ visit the holy sites of Jerusalem
- ❑ make the first day of the month the day to try a new, exotic recipe
- ❑ re-create our first date
- ❑ do leaf rubbings of the trees in my yard
- ❑ learn to identify animal tracks
- ❑ search for artifacts from the Viking colony of Vinland
- ❑ do not let my possessions "own" me
- ❑ stage a fashion show
- ❑ wear long-hair extensions and play Lady Godiva
- ❑ undertake an urban reforestation project in my city
- ❑ trace a love message in the sand
- ❑ find two tickets to Paris under my pillow
- ❑ get all new socks
- ❑ hold a theme dinner

- ❑ take a freighter from New Orleans to Buenos Aires
- ❑ be asked to make the commencement address at my former high school
- ❑ sail the Black Sea Passage through the Bosporus, the Sea of Marmara, and the Dardanelles
- ❑ ....
- ❑ ....
- ❑ ....
- ❑ ....
- ❑ attend the Philadelphia Flower Show
- ❑ build a greenhouse and have fresh vegetables year-round
- ❑ do my own basic car maintenance
- ❑ wish on a star
- ❑ participate in a windsurfing regatta
- ❑ eat steak-and-kidney pie in England
- ❑ scuba dive in Pearl Harbor
- ❑ not have to work
- ❑ start an alternative school with no separate classes

- ❏ ....
- ❏ ....
- ❏ ride the Très Grand Vitesse (TGV) from Brussels to Paris
- ❏ have free phone service
- ❏ drink espresso at night and still fall asleep
- ❏ be in the audience of *Late Night With David Letterman*
- ❏ attend a Willie Nelson concert
- ❏ see the Royal Ballet perform at Covent Garden in London
- ❏ own a virtual pet
- ❏ live near a great Chinese restaurant
- ❏ escape with my lover to a secluded ski lodge in the forests of Norway
- ❏ take the family on a learning vacation
- ❏ see giraffes mating in the wild
- ❏ live in a place where the summer never comes
- ❏ live in a place where the winter never comes
- ❏ make s'mores

❏ write my life story
❏ become an emergency medical technician
❏ ....
❏ ....
❏ ....
❏ walk dogs for the animal shelter
❏ paint my toenails
❏ go to a major league soccer match
❏ compose a mournful ballad
❏ buy season tickets to the ballet
❏ line the walkway to my house with
    luminaria
❏ spend a summer at a writer's colony
❏ try to paint the scudding movement of
    clouds
❏ be road manager for a rock group on tour
❏ start a publishing firm
❏ help conduct a census
❏ compile a life list of botanical specimens
❏ own a lucky horseshoe
❏ learn from experts
❏ take a creativity workshop

- ❑ tour the Coors Brewing Company in Golden, Colorado
- ❑ read Descartes' *Discourse on Method*
- ❑ improve my word power by doing the *Reader's Digest* word test every month
- ❑ walk across England
- ❑ not just alter my life but transform it
- ❑ make a finger ring out of a dollar bill
- ❑ build a sand city
- ❑ tie an unbreakable knot
- ❑ ....
- ❑ ....
- ❑ ....
- ❑ blindfold my lover and take him to a surprise destination
- ❑ bake an 18-grain bread
- ❑ master the game of charades
- ❑ make sure I do something I enjoy once a week
- ❑ operate a worm farm
- ❑ make the perfect crêpe Suzette
- ❑ winter on the Aleutian Islands

❑ be in the stands at the Daytona 500
❑ be appointed U.S. ambassador to the
     United Nations
❑ ....
❑ ....
❑ ....
❑ own a marble egg
❑ give up cooking
❑ be in Samoa for the rising of the coral reef
     worm known as the palolo, a delicacy
     considered "the caviar of the Pacific"
❑ master my moods
❑ be the most popular person in the office
❑ exchange lives with someone in Australia
     for a year
❑ stay up past my bedtime
❑ sharpen an ax
❑ attend an English country house weekend
❑ drive a classic MGA roadster
❑ be the first pick in the player draft
❑ write yet another version of the Romeo and
     Juliet story

- ❑ drive a Formula 1 car on a Grand Prix track
- ❑ dress in top hat, white tie, and tails
- ❑ plow a field
- ❑ bodysurf in Waimea Bay
- ❑ start a food fight
- ❑ know how to imitate bird calls
- ❑ divest my life of the superfluous
- ❑ produce a hit movie
- ❑ tour Oxford and Cambridge universities in England
- ❑ write a textbook that becomes the standard
- ❑ ....
- ❑ ....
- ❑ clean out the attic
- ❑ go on an Earthwatch vacation where I really contribute
- ❑ travel to all 50 states
- ❑ have a lifetime supply of honey from Mérida, Mexico
- ❑ kayak the Nantahala River in North Carolina

- ❏ memorize Shelley's "Ode to the Western Wind"
- ❏ attend the New Orleans Jazz & Heritage Festival
- ❏ try an extreme sport
- ❏ be a person others can rely on
- ❏ interview Charlie Rose
- ❏ campaign for closed-captioning of all public media, including the Internet
- ❏ buy all new sheets and towels—none of them white
- ❏ own a vintage Cadillac Fleetwood
- ❏ ....
- ❏ ....
- ❏ ....
- ❏ ....
- ❏ drink only branch water with my bourbon
- ❏ be a good friend to my friends
- ❏ create and name a new color
- ❏ be able to identify woodland plants
- ❏ participate in the monthlong Muslim holiday of Ramadan

- ❏ get the morning paper delivered
- ❏ eat a dozen blue point oysters at the Acme Oyster Bar in New Orleans
- ❏ lose my tendency to blush
- ❏ keep my word
- ❏ swim with David Hasselhof
- ❏ scale an indoor climbing wall
- ❏ hold a press conference
- ❏ see the remains of the Minoan palace at Herakleion, Crete
- ❏ stop procrastinating
- ❏ avoid splitting an infinitive
- ❏ install track lighting in my dining room
- ❏ avoid all fats
- ❏ grow a lemon tree in a pot indoors
- ❏ own a pair of Adirondack chairs for summers on the deck
- ❏ eat brown-bag lunches at work
- ❏ create a rooftop garden for my apartment building
- ❏ be honest about who I am
- ❏ pick a century and study all aspects of it

❑ buy all I want in a stationery store

❑ ....

❑ ....

❑ ....

❑ drive a taxi

❑ paint a still life

❑ sleep under a blanket of apple blossoms

❑ have an action figure done in my likeness

❑ travel to Mongolia

❑ never wait in line for a movie

❑ spend weekends at my country house

❑ cover my walls with textured fabric

❑ get a perm

❑ spend a week in Branson, Missouri, for
    fishing all day and a live show each night

❑ play badminton without apologizing

❑ live on the 30th floor

❑ start a fashion trend

❑ learn to play soccer

❑ be appointed ambassador to India

❑ go back in time to be in the audience when
    Caruso and Ponselle are singing

- ❑ speak five languages
- ❑ own every Billie Holliday recording
- ❑ see Bigfoot
- ❑ celebrate someone's new job by giving them a fancy pen-and-pencil desk set
- ❑ read *Don Quixote*
- ❑ work behind the scenes on Madonna's next world tour
- ❑ stage an Audrey Hepburn film festival
- ❑ eat junk food while perusing a trash magazine
- ❑ ....
- ❑ ....
- ❑ ....
- ❑ own a pair of Mephistos
- ❑ campaign to save Oregon's coho salmon
- ❑ see a production of Aeschylus's *Oresteia*
- ❑ cast a sculpture in bronze
- ❑ stay at the landmark Pioneer Inn in Lahaina, Maui
- ❑ ride the 20th Century Limited in a private compartment

❑ start a recycling business to make luxury
    fabrics out of plastic

❑ ....

❑ ....

❑ ....

❑ ....

❑ visit the 15th-century Gobelin tapestry
    workshop in Paris

❑ understand the American West by reading
    Wallace Stegner

❑ visit the site of Jamestown, Virginia, first
    permanent English colony in America

❑ own a small Hepplewhite table with inlaid
    decoration

❑ get a see-through shower curtain

❑ telephone the one person I've always been
    afraid to call—and get it over with

❑ be known for habitually using a particular
    catchphrase

❑ when reading a great book, restrict
    myself to ten pages a day to prolong
    the pleasure

- ☐ ....
- ☐ ....
- ☐ ....
- ☐ ....
- ☐ shop for soapstone sculptures in the Inuit villages of Baffin Island
- ☐ see the Palio in Siena, Italy, the annual horserace event played out in period costume and according to medieval rules
- ☐ husband my resources and keep something in reserve
- ☐ see all my wishes come true
- ☐ be careful what I wish for

ABOUT THE AUTHOR

Barbara Ann Kipfer is the author of the bestselling book, *14,000 Things To Be Happy About.* She is Head Lexicographer of Associative Computing, Inc., working with artificial intelligence systems. She holds a Ph.D. in linguistics and is currently completing a Ph.D. in archeology. Dr. Kipfer has published twelve reference books, including *Roget's 21st-Century Thesaurus.* She recently moved with her family to a town in Connecticut, where she has always wished to live.